Paranormalization

Memoirs of an Academic Layperson

Ron Yacovetti

Foreword by
Johnny Zaffis

BEYOND THE FRAY
Publishing

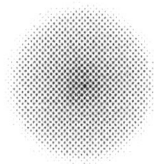

BEYOND THE FRAY

Publishing

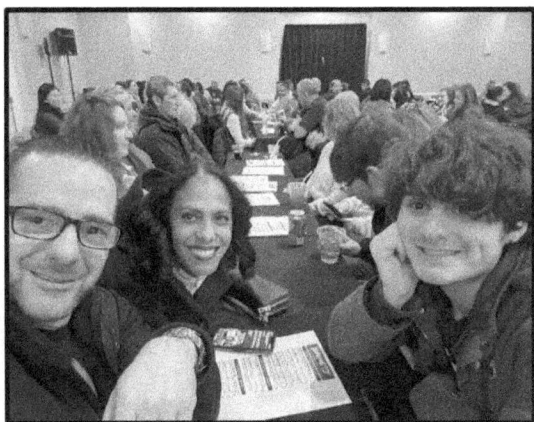

As is the case with every book I do, as well as for everything I've ever done, my dad has stood behind me, so this book is dedicated to him and the Olympic-high-jump level of excellence as a dad and as a human being that he has set as an example for me. Also, to my loving son, Antonio, who inspires me with his intellect, caring and wit already at the age of sixteen. And to my beautiful girlfriend and DRV partner, Lourdes Gonzalez, whom I continue to love and value her input in all of our spirit contact and life endeavors. And additionally, I wanted to note a special place in my life for Mr. Tony Rathman, who not only took up the mantle of DRV alongside his beautiful wife, Cherie, in concert with Lourdes *and me, but who also set a standard of excellence in friendship, loyalty and brilliance that reminds me how people can be respectable and respectful, successful and sincere and all while treating others with genuine care and consideration... all of the time. Together, the four of us shall shake the very foundation of ITC and spirit communication, to the degree that it is uplifting to those who work at the cause of validity and authenticity and, equally so, sending palpable and impossible to ignore tremors out to those who feel that they stand on the solid materialist grounds of doubt. Quaked, rattled and rolled, folks!*

Contents

Foreword by Johnny Zaffis   ix

Introduction   xi

About DRV: Direct Radio Voice   xiii

1. No Iron(y) Deficiency   1
2. Cheap Carpets Atop Hardwood Floors   19
3. The Grokking Dead   25
4. Superluminal: Faster Than the Speed of Light?!   33
5. The Philip Experiment   43
6. The Hypocrisy of Temporized Telegraphy   55
7. Consciously Ignoring Consciousness?!   61
8. Shifting the Debate: Belief in Consciousness vs. Ghosts   71
9. Bye-Bye Bias: Research Has No Place for You   81
10. Fantastical Feats of the Layperson   87
11. Down Goes Tyson!   93
12. Am I Qualia-Fied?   103
13. Brother, Can You Spare a (Para)Dime?   109
14. ITC's Prominent Methodologies   121
15. We Win AND Lose by Knockout!?   125
16. The Voices of Entity Voices   131
17. Life Is But a Dream?   149
18. Frank-ly Speaking About Spirit   157
19. If It's All in My Head, Why Am I Not Making It Easy?!   167
20. Artificial Intelligence and the Chinese Room   173
21. Annotations, Assumptions and A-holes   179

About the Author   185
Also by Ron Yacovetti   187

Foreword by Johnny Zaffis
"The Godfather of the Paranormal"

I have had the opportunity to work with Ron Yacovetti at several historical locations that have reported paranormal activity within their walls. The Shanley Hotel and the Conjuring House are just two that I have worked with Ron, and I can say without any doubt, his passion for doing this work is definitely in the forefront with documenting the activity and hoping it will bring a better understanding to many in the field of research. His work is proving the theories out, and the repeatability is what is needed in the paranormal field.

Today I am very glad I have had the opportunity to see and witness Ron's work with instrumental transcommunication (ITC) and developing ways to use old methods along with the new ones to prove out what so many of us have in theory in the world of the supernatural. I hope Ron's investigating, passion and love for this field will live on for a long time and that his work continues with a variety of equipment and people looking for the research into the afterlife, leaving no area unexplored; the possibilities are endless within this field.

So open up your mind, as the possibilities are endless, for the gaining of knowledge is power.

Johnny Zaffis

Introduction

What and How Is a State of Paranormalization Reached?

Paranormal: Things that are beyond the scope of normal scientific understanding.

1. (Sociology): The process through which ideas and behaviors that may fall outside of social norms come to be regarded as "normal."
2. **Author's note: The rate at which these paranormal occurrences happen, and to the number of people worldwide that they do, now begs the question of whether or not experiencing them OR NOT experiencing them is the most supported position to be labeled "normal."**
3. (Data-based) The process of organizing data in a database. This includes creating tables and establishing relationships between those tables according to rules designed both to protect the data

and to make the database more flexible by eliminating redundancy and inconsistent dependency.

Paranormalization: Think of the birthing of the peanut butter cup- one fell into the other and BAM!...something worth sinking one's teeth into emerges...and eventually finds strong commercial presence in society. Oh yeah, I just went there – candy branding and ghosty stuff, and we're just getting started here.

Summary: When regardless of bias, belief or lack of experience, we accept as a worldview that this stuff happens and look at causality, repeatability and the anthropological facets of it. We've graduated beyond "IF"! Perhaps we're on the precipice of realizing that the only reason what we deem to be paranormal seems beyond the norm is because we are only aware and educated enough, as a people, to the appetizers section of all things reality. If one expands their property and its footprint, what exists outside of their space previously may then exist within their comfort zone.

About DRV: Direct Radio Voice

Direct radio voice, or as our world of acronyms would come to know it, DRV, is a methodology of spirit communication known to too few despite its early and significant roots. At a time when small factions in varying parts of the world were being inculcated into communing with spirits using equipment and no longer being limited to Ouija boards and mediums, all spiritual vocal evidence was categorized as EVP, <u>electronic voice phenomena</u>.

A handful of the pioneers in Europe not only began recording anomalous vocals using magnetic wire, analog, reel to reel and eventually digital recording devices, they also introduced the practice of applying a form of noise, white noise, to function as audio support in order to make these undetectable voices more discernable and clearer to understand. Their regular spirit communicators would provide technical advice, inevitably speaking to the onset of our now burgeoning age of electronics. Their messages spoke of the use of a radio on a vacant radio frequency within the more fundamentally prone to interference AM band, pointing out that the progression of this would lead to the voices coming out through the radios themselves. This concept, as we now know, is undoubtedly what happened. The voices from beyond that we deem as the voices of spirit were facilitating contact using our military-, consumer- and professional-grade radios. In the mid-1990s German physicist Dr. Ernst Senkowski decided that we needed a term to delineate between EVP, which is record and review, and real-time dialog with spirit, live in the moment. This new offshoot electronic method would be termed ITC, instrumental transcommunication. DRV is its earliest offspring and arguably its most accomplished.

With the booming paranormal landscape, in large part due to television shows that began to flood the airways, ITC did get noticed, but the means of doing it had taken a turn. The late, brilliant Frank Sumption had created a way to sweep through broadcast radio channels with the idea that entities (aliens were his first target audience) would be able to use the randomized fragments of sound to form audible words. And while this method does work, DRV became a lost art, relegated to a very minute few, none of whom were a part of this American media-driven ghost-hunting frenzy. Spirit boxes, ghost boxes and the like became synonymous with ITC despite the fact that they were almost posthumously rising to notoriety as DRV faded into a European chapter of paranormal history. But in 2019, I had an epiphany moment...and then Lourdes Gonzalez and I, inspired by ITC and DRV icon Dr. Anabela Cardoso as well as Marcello Bacci, resurrected this lost art of spirit communication and developed it over the next few years. In time, we would find ourselves collaborating with ITC great Tony Rathman and his wife, Cherie, in the aggressive campaign to take DRV into the next level of real-time spirit contact...again, which is what ITC was coined to be. The method uses pure white noise. Period. No human vocal fragments, no broadcast vocals whatsoever, and no sweep. The channel, be it longwave, medium wave or shortwave AM, is barren of all signs of human speech.

Lourdes and I, along with Tony and Cherie, continue to experiment with ways to maximize the length and quality of contact with the spirit realm. Some of our greatest innovations to this method, which itself was born in an evolutionary way, have become revolutionary in their application. From the generating of new and controlled live white noise devoid of any radio, removing the low-hanging fruit of the cynic to suggest, fueled by bias, that stray radio voices were bleeding into the recordings, to the out-of-the-box concept of actually slowing down live white noise in real time, the results are nothing shy of extraordinary. DRV, as we have developed it today, can be and is being done without any of the characteristics that cynics and closed-minded academics frown on about ITC.

Added to that, we are doing it with a shift in protocol, taking the cleaning up of noise via filtration, the normalizing of sound, and the act of slowing it down in real time, which collectively and essentially is taking the review portion of audio capture and infusing it live during the recording of the given DRV session. DRV, direct radio voice, is not a box, it is not a device, it is a methodology that today in 2023 is seeing a rebirth while it continues to blaze a path that will grow increasingly more difficult to ignore or deny. Today, this method has evolved into "the Staticom Project," with the employing of pure live white noise generated in the very moment within which contact with spirit is being made. Much more on that later in this book!

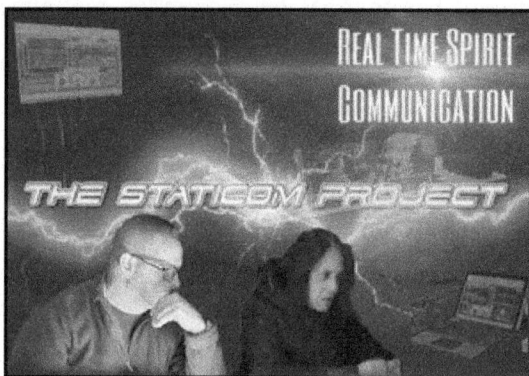

1. No Iron(y) Deficiency
You Can't Trust YOUR Senses, but You CAN Trust Mine?

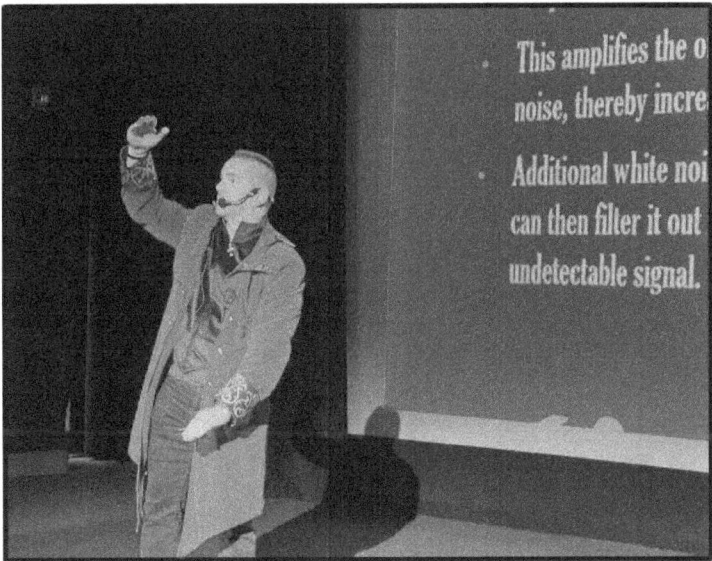

Wait...What?!

CERTAINLY NO ONE actually says those words to us paranormalists. Well, I can't say for sure if it has ever been or never been said, but I can speak with absolute certainty that IT IS IMPLIED through commentary and never loses its boundlessly offensive absurdity. I wish I were making this up for humorous effect or something along those lines, but I am not. And I cannot believe the revolt of researchers who deal with this baloney has not risen up and started to squash it. I am not rebelling against alternate opinions, criticisms, or the individual right to doubt. But I am flustered by the irony-laden statements that are slung at members of our community like a table with no legs: can't stack anything on it, considering there are no legs to stand on. I'll explain...(and you knew I would).

The very basic version or summary of what I am saying is this...that the paranormal investigator or researcher comes to conclusions based on their sensory interpretations of proposed evidence of paranormality, and the hard-core cynic says that they are wrong and misconstruing noise and audio artifacts, all the while coming to adverse opinions and determining there is NO spiritual influence at play, both blaming and using the same biological and physiological bodily tools. Go ahead and read that as many times as necessary to get more offended, more clear, or more confused by this accepted dynamic between two sides of a coin that say that they seek the truth.

Short version of what these people are saying, whether they know it or admit it, is..."your ears and eyes suck and falter heavily in accuracy, and I should know because mine are superior, more efficient and damn near flawless in their functionality...oh, and by the way, they are biologically and essentially identical to yours...but you know, better."

Added to this is the fact that IF they denounce and deny the claim noted above, suggesting that they have superior biological auditory tools and skills, then they are forced to pull the ripcord on the parachute of bias in order to save them from a crash-and-burn scenario. Because the simple fact is that if we have equal footing to be correct or incorrect based on our physiological ability to hear and process sound, and we rule out and factor in details such as age, gender, etc., then you end up with their superiority in the audio capture actually being fully rooted in belief.

If they are operating out of the accepted reductionist, materialist view of science where no paranormality exists, then the battle of the ear skills goes to the one on the side of the masses...right? Right? No, huh? Of course not. Facts and preponderance of evidence don't care about the masses, clicks, likes or followers.

Adding more fuel to this fire of spontaneous fool combustion is that in order to be forced into standing upon the platform of belief and mass agreement among others, you toss out the baby of science with the filthiest of bathwater. Science, as Dr. Rupert Sheldrake so eloquently puts it, "...is a method of inquiry. Not an ideology." So one cannot hold the title of scientific and biased believer concurrently. That's like declaring oneself a vegan all week with a routine Saturday hamburger between the workweeks.

Essentially what this scenario shows us, both from within ourselves or from an outside observer view, is that we need data to show our work; and not data to support superiority but to show specificity in hearing, processing and analysis.

An example being a higher frequency recorded vocal and the assessment of it being paranormal being by a male over fifty years old, the range at which men start to experience a decline in higher-frequency hearing. Yes, I am among them – I'm sorry, what was that you said? Huh? Speak up already... Kidding. I hear you...figuratively.

My point here is that we, as a society overall and certainly as a community of paranormalists, have gotten comfortable laying down statements with all of the support of a tinderbox under an elephant. We heard it on TV, we heard it from a guy or lady who looked smart or the big one, we read it online, and BAM...it's fact. Truth is, what you read or witness may very well be, but you should always take the extra step or so and vet it, be sure of it, and know that even if you end up being wrong, that you did some due diligence to be sure your odds of being educated were exercised first.

Now, as I am always more than willing to admit, I am not a scientist, nor do I hold a PhD in anything. I have a BA in communications (see? College was worth it) and have done a lot of what those who do attain those degrees do...read, study and experiment a lot. The truth is, and I love this term, likely coined by the brilliant Tom Butler (also not a PhD), I do feel that in the community of ghost hunters, I am one of those who would be viewed as an "academic layperson." Mr. Butler wrote about this in a very declarative and truth-revealing manner. There is what he terms an "Academic-Layperson partition" – the gap between those of the highest education and deepest familiarity with scientific method and practices, and on the other side of the solidified barrier are those who are on the paranormal front lines aggregating the lion's share of all paranormal data and alleged evidence. So actual research and experimentation that is not geared towards clicks and likes and the visual sensationalism, that is where you build up a body of respectable work. The main problem, as I see it from my nonscientist perspective, is that those who are of science are not doing the amount of paranormal experimenting, if any, and if they are, they still need to be truly scientific in seeking truth and not filling a biased-driven agenda like a cheap CVS prescription. When bias is driving the vehicle, it is never on course. We all possess some, and it is ok, like skepticism, to be an ingredient, but if a strong pro or con belief system supersedes or colors one's interpretation or willingness to accept details, then that throws the PhD right out the window, to me. Hitler had brilliant scientists on his horrific domination-quest team, their education and pedigree academically could not make any of those atrocities justifiable or ok on any level. None. So there is an extreme example of my point – humanity and altruism need to be in line, and a fancy cap, gown and alma mater does not make anyone always correct.

How fallible or accurate is, or should, one's hearing be?

Is there a standard for common traits and drawbacks in hearing applicable to all of us? Can we build theory on the ideas and data should such exist?

Here's a societal importance mind-bender for you all. As most of those who would be reading any of my books would know, many of us in the field of paranormal investigating or research do not do it as our vocation, not as our full-time jobs. This is nothing of a discrediting nature, even though I am sure some may see it as such. The same way our lives and society have evolved to where most households rely upon two incomes, many personal and professional endeavors are not our only, if at all, source of income. I always loved the positive mindset affirmations that in essence say that when you do something part-time, but the impression others have is that you do it full-time, THAT is how you hustle and maximize your life and its passion. For a lot of us who began as hunters of ghosts on our journeys to present day, we have many convinced, in large part with the help of social media and its round-the-clock availability, that we do our paranormal thing constantly, every weekend, every month, just nonstop, to the point that they occasionally ask how we make time to work, see our kids and, well, write books. It isn't even a second thought when you have time and passion.

A great example from my personal life is how five days a week, at my day job, I spend my lunch hour reviewing audio, editing video, writing my books, and even running DRV and Staticom sessions in quiet, back-room office spaces. Almost everyone else I work with steps out for lunch, especially when the winter has had its time and the warmth and sunshine of the northeast spring and summer set in. Outside is way better than going from the work computer to one's own computer and from one desk in the office space to another one. But for me, the time is a gift, and the feelings brought forth from completing a project are hard to compete with, even for the sun. I digress...

So...when you take into account that so many of us have trades or careers outside of the paranormal realm, you have to wonder how many of those jobs provide the investigator or researcher a set of skills that are extremely useful for all things ghostly.

As two immediate examples that come to mind, from our podcast, running three years now, *Entity Voices Paranormal Evidence*, Chris Allgood and my partner, Lourdes Gonzalez, BOTH have very viable trade skills when it comes to all things paranormal.

Chris Allgood has worked over twenty years with construction, especially with windows and doors. I cannot tell you how many podcasts that we have done where he is able to speak to visual evidence with detail and extreme relevance that no one else on the episode, including the guest investigator, could've possibly addressed. Dimensions, functionality, date and time period authenticity of windows and doors, not to mention what they could have (or not) possibly attributed to with regard to sounds or anomalous movements on their own. It is a lesson on situational awareness, as we often mention with regard to Chris, but even more so on educational awareness. One cannot speak to or observe those things unless they are even aware of those details. Huge skillset with what we do at historic locations. We are certainly grateful for his presence on the shows and the rare moments, due to geographic situations, that we have been able to work in the field together.

Now, even more to the bullseye on this evidence stuff, with regard to audio and whether or not we need a national poll to decide if our ears are doing ok, is my partner and girlfriend, Lourdes Gonzalez. Her trade skills are an immense advantage with review and assessment of audio because she is, by trade, a court reporter. I am not sure there is a better vocation to educate one's hearing and ability to discern speech than court reporting. I cannot tell you how many times I was at my desk and, from the kitchen, she walks over and says, "Rewind that audio...play that again...it says..." and what she thinks it says, IT SAYS! To me, this is a MAJOR LEAGUE big deal because knowing how sound works, how audio behaves, how to produce sound is all important...BUT when the advanced skillset or dare I say, expertise, is in LISTENING to sound, listening for speech, in linguistics, well then, that, my friends, is a pinnacle amongst those skills. If you give me the option to argue with a court reporter or parapsychologist about what an anomalous vocal may be saying, give me that parapsychologist and their Ivy League PhD any day, because that's bush league compared to how these stenographer folks biologically process sound and speech input.

Lourdes listens on a daily basis and is paid to do so, listening for hours to rooms full of people testifying in courts of law. Physics has its laws, and so do societies. Add to that it entails listening to and for vast variations in cadence, tone, emphasis, pattern, volume, people talking over each other, one voice finishes as another picks up the very next available syllable and starts a new thought. It is insane.

I love how having a background in engineering audio can sometimes be used as a trump card in telling someone that they are hearing audio artifacts and warbles of sound and not actual talking or dialog, which in SO MANY instances is like telling someone that their ability to run quickly is mostly due to the brand of athletic shoes they've purchased. Absurd, yes! And should not so easily be dismissed with the simplicity of a blanket statement and the lack of experience with the collection of evidence, limited to only having seen and heard three minutes of one clip.

So listen, academic elite who judge so quickly, on the strength of JUST ONE video clip, telling folks that they are hearing warbles and artifacts that somehow form a cohesive message over a minute long...BECAUSE...and hear me...I HAVE A COURT REPORTER. Her expertise is qualified to tell all of us whether or not YOUR assessment of OUR audio is accurate or unfounded, other than when judged by bias, of course.

If we're going to judge and evaluate credibility based on what "lanes" we need to stay in, determined by our limitations of knowledge, skill and experience, then do not be so comfortable challenging an expert within a territory you do not possess the same feather-filled cap, and take a page from the mastery of a court reporter on audio assessments. Damn, that feels good making sense and sharing it with those in need of it.

That all said, let us look at the "scientific process" of peer review and studies that tell us how things are not what we think because four out of five dentists did not hear the same thing. A majority does not make something correct. It is democratic as processes go, but it is not a direct correlation to correctness. We are led to believe that is so, but not in reality, no, it is not. It is important to me to note that in the dismissal of potential evidence of paranormality, mass-hysteria-like group misconstruing of what happens is often applied, but when assessing the evidence, we somehow disband with the notion that THAT may itself be a mass delusion led by bias and scrutiny of others. So...tighten your seatbelt again...this is where it gets bumpy because I make it so. Heck, I like to shake the tree and provoke thought. If people feel provoked, that is on them. Perhaps thought isn't regular practice for them, and it offends them. I am not saying I am right, it's my way, or it's wrong. I am saying with conviction what I feel. I am supporting it, which leads to MY belief, and then serving it up for you to hopefully reflect upon it with your own experience. Here goes...I begin with a HUGE question.

Since when does a basic human function such as hearing need a mob-rule committee-like, collective agreement in order for an individual or small group of people to credibly be able to speak with the utmost confidence about WHAT THEY JUST HEARD?! Not to mention, which I dive into more later, their accepted, personal paradigm determines what data they will accept or reject, so they're evaluating what they already deem as impossible and absurd, yet their participation gives them the status of "objective test subject." Not fooling many of us with this empty-gesture protocol process.

Honestly, my inner satirist runs rampant with this whole "need a committee" concept of validating sensory input that I made it over fifty years assessing on my own crap! Think of the endless, senseless possibilities that it can take on if we buy into that idea as a reliable foundation for not only accepting paranormal audio evidence, but for hearing anything.

Take this scenario, for example, a jury deliberates, comes to a decision, a representative of the jury speaks aloud in court and states what that decision is, so...according to the lack of reliability imbued within human hearing, which is not at all biased towards the paranormal (coughing on sarcasm), we would then need another twelve-person jury to be brought in to determine if all of the people in the courtroom, judge included, actually heard the same verdict of "guilty," "not guilty" or something else completely different. We can't just ask them...they will say what they heard, and in our unbiased theory on human hearing, not at all skewed against the paranormal, that honest response from a person isn't something we can count on. See why I love and apply continuity of thought to my own work and to the stuff the field and all of its members, agreeable or not with my mindset, ask me to buy into? Sometimes, like success (and this is an example of one, to me), if you see things through long enough, you begin to see the contradictions, flaws and full picture with the application of a thought process or mentality. In our physical sensory world, fire is always hot. There is no icy-cold fire that burns down a house. As Dr. Charles Tart always says, "data is king." And that attribute of fire is universally accepted. Perhaps our para-field should look to apply such continuity to its practices, theories and judgments.

Below is a prime example of a questionnaire from a website that is posting a different methodology than ITC, noting its own (self-assessed) advantages and noting the laundry list of "NO" answers when it comes to ITC. The problem with that is that it is scientistic not scientific. In saying such, meaning each line/question, it presupposes that either there is only

ONE means of or method of ITC and it fails to meet these criteria…OR…that there are multiple means of performing ITC and that they all fall short equally and identically. I doubt the latter is the case, and lean much more into the concept of this all judging ITC by its brand extraordinaire and biggest target for cynicism, the sweeping ghost box. After each point, I will refute, respond and rectify things as a sub-point in *italics*.

- Experiments done at accredited university –
  Website answer = No.

  Anomalous vocals can be captured anywhere. Locations may or may not aid in the process. If the location is a concern due to trusted implementation of control, then start wrangling up those anthropologists, astronomers and their planets and do THAT work inside a university building too. Field sciences are recognized. Proper protocol matters, not home-field advantage. We won't even declare a location haunted purely on the strength of capturing anomalous voices since we can attain them anywhere.

- Proper controls used during research – **Website answer = No.**

  There is actually someone confident enough to speak to an entire field of study (ITC) and address every instance ever performed and say "NO"? Arrogance meet your maker – holy sh*t!

- Experimental methods shared with others –
  Website answer = Not always.

If not shared, how can anyone evaluate it with regard to proper controls? If you don't know what is being done to conduct an ITC session, how can you say protocol isn't being followed? ANY protocol. One cannot condemn a movie one did not sit through and watch. Come on now. Maybe some researchers don't wish to see their method hijacked and taken credit for or ripped apart by carnivorous peers looking to sink their teeth into something they fear is superior. Possible...quite possible. And hey, it is beyond safe to say that the ones not sharing are simply not sharing with these questionnaire folks.

3. Experimental methods shared with others	Yes	Not Always
3. Experimental methods shared with others	Yes	No

- Experimental methods shared with others –
  Website answer = No.

This EXACT question is listed TWICE, with two different answers on behalf of ITC, and BOTH listed as question #3. This is who is judging harshly the accuracy of data being logged, acquired and our protocols? And besides...if this is a statement about ghost boxes, someone needs to go online to eBay, Amazon and a variety of ghost-themed sites that build and sell the equipment. Now if attaining one of those and using it is not enough because you cannot deconstruct or dissect it to know how it works and should work, then perhaps you're already playing above your league of quali-

fication damning the boxes as a whole. If this refers to DRV, then it is just silly. The method is available to read about. At its core, it uses a vacant AM station, and you record your dialog with spirit. Now if this is also too elusive a path to find in preparation for statements such as "Methods shared with others," then you really are being lazy.

- Replicated results obtained by persons besides primary investigator – **Website answer = No**.

Blanket statements seem to be a thing here amongst this list. And in my personal experience with ITC and most specifically DRV and Staticom, I replicated my full configuration for our partner Tony Rathman, and he was able to attain vocals, make improvements, and uphold the consistency of them at the level I myself had been producing. Also, some others began trying to replicate the Staticom method and seem to be producing voices as well.

- Results published in peer-reviewed scientific journals – **Website answer = No.**

There are, on Academia.com alone, papers on ITC both in favor of and skeptical about the methods in play in the field. Since I am an obvious proponent for it, I will make a declaration from that perspective and mention the amazing Dr. Anabela Cardoso, who has papers on there, for peer review and comments, discussion and disclosure. In all fairness, in concept I do like this forum for all things new and possibly groundbreaking. But...bias runs rampant, and instead of a healthy discussion, it often ends up tantamount to bloody fish in shark-infested waters, just observing the varying depths that others take a bite out of it. So, in the mindset of the skeptic needs to be right one hundred percent of the time or they are not right at all, this line item of the judgy kind is an epic fail.

- Significant findings obtained from the research – **Website answer = No.**

In whose opinion? Not mine nor thousands in the field of paranormal research. Now, this may just be me, being an educated layperson, but when you qualify data with an adjective, you leave things open to the concept of interpretation. I myself have recorded sessions that, be it viewed as having led to an immense success, or as to what one who blames it all on warbles and artifacts would see as a huge misconstruing of noise, that...by definition and the ruling out of options in pursuit of real answers, IS significant!

- Consistent findings observed – **Website answer = No.**

Ignoring data does not a vanishing act make. In many of my own and my colleagues' experiences in ITC work, findings have been quite consistent. The fact that some of us see the findings as anomalous vocals that defy explanation and others may, with limited attention paid to them, dismiss them as misinterpreted noises does not indicate that those findings did not happen consistently. As a matter of fact if the above lines of question alone, in their refuting of ITC, are not founded in the assessment OF findings...then the lazy and the ignorant have fused like a peanut butter tub that chocolate accidentally fell into, accidentally but not so sweet as the delectable example given here. Actually leaves a bad taste in one's mouth.

- Experimenter has PhD or other scientific research degrees from reputable and established universities – **Website answer = No.**

Now, while this has its merits, and it can be a sign of a variety of critical things, if a method in use, if a methodology applied properly yields voices that are inexplicable, it is not directly related to the institutional certificate, affiliation and status that the operator has spent a fortune on. Marcello Bacci achieved amazing results in ITC. The spirit realm, assuming that anyone making contact attempts believes it to be real, surely does not do a collegiate prescreening before using a remarkable method of communicating between realms. So why is it we're discussing this? Ah yes, personal credibility. This would, to me, be more pertinent if we were discussing the construction and engineering of equipment for communication. Today's ghost box builders ARE brilliant, whether you fancy the methodology or not. So then, what this question begs us to ask is, "Are we comfortable suggesting that no one from an elite school with a lofty degree is a candidate for error, deception and bias? Only those of the highest of education and the premier schools can make a ghost talk through a method of contact?" – Has America's Got Talent taught us nothing? The general public CAN and WILL amaze you! This isn't even like shooting fish in a barrel...it's like shooting the freaking barrel. Next...

- Based on contemporary electro-magnetic field theory – **Website answer = No.**

Now, to my knowledge, and I do take pride in knowing a lot of what spirit contact has done, tried, and failed in doing, we cannot be sure that this is happening, that this is a prerequisite, and that this makes any difference. My only question is, "Does contemporary electromagnetic field theory exclude electronics and signals such as RF and any use of white noise?" BY definition via Google, it says that... "Electromagnetic fields are a combination of invisible electric and magnetic fields of force. They are generated by natural phenomena like the Earth's magnetic field but also by human activities, mainly through the use of electricity." Seems to me radio use, white-noise generator use, and audio processes would fall within that definition. How much of a factor the Earth's forces play or any natural and invisible forces as well, I believe remains speculative at best. If someone does know with certainty, then they should read that "doesn't share" section that came before this and start sharing it.

Holy crap was that tedious because it is like explaining the same basic concept to a toddler, when to you, the adult, it seems so elementary in nature. This is not any attempt on my part, nor my teammates', to cast insults towards the intellect of others who do research. Oh contraire...to me, those people who composed the questions I just ran through, they are probably higher in IQ and brilliant in so many ways...BUT... and I say this constantly...when bias is behind the wheel, a righteous path you cannot find or follow. The questions leave too much room for interpretation and rely way too much on blanketed opinions and conclusions, born of a very limited percentage of what is being addressed. Very. The structure of the questions also does less than an adequate job in hiding its agenda to notably distance its authors and affiliates from the area of spiritual communication known as ITC. Let's get a few of those parapsychologists on their retainer to perhaps tackle the persistent problem in society that causes so many to diminish others in order to experience inner growth and elevation, to experience a strong sense of accomplishment. My resurrecting DRV in the era of the ghost box put me in a fringe group at risk of isolation, for sure. And with ghost box builders for over a decade, like Tony Rathman, who no longer even conducts sessions with any of his boxes, the conversion to a DRV-minded approach hits even harder.

In my perfect world in my little head, an acknowledgment of the successes and failures of other methods is paramount in making any case for spirit contact, or you leave yourself open to field a plethora of "what about" questions born out of lists like the one above. Deep breath...moving on.

2. Cheap Carpets Atop Hardwood Floors

Why Reverence and Respect for Those Before Us Matters

Oᴋ, even for the open-minded and creative types, this chapter title may be causing some bewilderment. Like, seriously, dude (said to me in your mind), what in the world does

that, could that, and should that mean? Listen, people...I
don't blame you. If I am honest, and I am, it was a non-paranormal moment that I was experiencing when this metaphorical epiphany hit me. Allow me to explain...or try...here
goes...

This idea came to me when looking back at those who did
what I do, similarly or differently, but for certain, their work
is an essential component of my work's foundation, inspira-
tion and groundbreaking outcomes. I have been told that I
give those pioneers in ITC more credit than I should, while
taking almost none (if any) for myself. I guess it's because I
understand that my path would not be MY path without the
influence and awareness of theirs. It just wouldn't.

Imagine, in essence, anytime you have been to a friend's or
someplace where they tore up some old and tattered carpet
only to discover, before actually replacing that with a newer
carpet, that there is this elegant, polished natural wood floor
beneath it. And it was there all along, maybe years, yet they
or you never knew it. THAT is what I feel we do when we
teach, preach and pontificate out in our field without some
verbal bibliography to show the proper respect to those we
should thank for making our efforts plausible and possible.
Nick Groff, pictured at the onset of this chapter, is no excep-
tion. He's a pioneer and a really kind, genuine soul.

So if you engage me in a conversation about ITC and especially DRV, you can expect it to be laden with reverence for
those before me. Now, I am not trying to play the humble
card (it'd be great if Las Vegas poker had one of these, lol) or

appear to be on some sort of altruistic quest for respect. This is a genuine thing to me that is not only emotionally driven when it is I who is giving proper kudos to my forefathers, but almost equally emotional when I see others who are building upon the legends before them yet seemingly making no mention of them, representing their impressive body of work as if birthed both in concept, proof of concept and execution. I am fully aware that there may be some whom I see as guilty of such, but because I am not privy to their every appearance and move, I do not see that I am wrong about them. In every possible instance of this, I hope I am wrong more than ever before, because I would hate to think good people are missing that idealistic concept of displaying reverence to the correct people.

One example I always think about, my knowledge of which is limited to a few experiences, is the now known "Paranormal Couple" of Cody Desbiens and Satori Hawes (yes, Jason's daughter) and their tapping and rapping communication methodology. I do not know if they call it by its original name, telegraphy, but in doing so, it would directly link it to those who first hit the supernatural scene with that strategy, the Fox sisters. In fact, those three psychical siblings really created that scene, forging the spiritualist movement that rages on to this day. Others used the method concurrently and subsequently, such as the Davenport brothers and Daniel Dunglas Home, but the Fox sisters are synonymous with its inception. Now, if this does get mentioned, brought up and shared at Cody and Satori's presentations, then let that serve as an example of how showing reverence for those before us looks. If they do not, one would assume it to be an oversight. Always try to give the benefit of the doubt, especially when it comes to kind people. And one thing I would say from personal experience is that the two of them ARE very nice and lovable people. And of course, I would think as the daughter of such a brilliant pioneer of the modern ghost-hunting movement, she would understand how important it is to practice this retrospective respect. Her father absolutely deserves it from many of us who started as or remain ghost hunters, which by name, Jason even helped make a household term.

It would be a shame if in a quest for notoriety and fame, it is ever portrayed as if invented by or stumbled upon as a divine intervention moment, obfuscating the spiritualists who did it before our era. And not to mention, most notably those of our modern ghost-hunting population, whom I have found in my own radio communication endeavors and interactions, are oftentimes in no way familiar with ITC and DRV greats such as Marcello Bacci.

Hell, I wonder how many people who call themselves an ITC guy or gal even know that the term was coined in the 1980s by German physicist Dr. Ernst Senkowski. I bet those who don't know the founder of the term ITC DO know who is responsible for founding KFC...the colonel, of course. Colonel Sanders. But Dr. Senkowski, if by chance, not so much, may speak to the level of awareness and reverence toward those who came before. If you possess the ability to raise one eyebrow in doubt, now would be the time to do it. I can't, or I'd be right there with ya on it. And hey, this is no slinging of poo at anyone – this, like any of our life's short-comings, is an opportunity to make it right, correct it, and be in a better place on the subject. One cannot declare themself a baseball fan and, as I've mentioned before, simultaneously only know Babe Ruth to be a candy bar. If you invent or pioneer something, call it what it is. If you build upon the work, progress and experimentation of those before you, many of whom may no longer be present in the flesh to speak on their own behalf, you speak for them, about them and most critically with the utmost respect and acknowledgment. We owe to them, at least as much, to forbid the history of spirit communication from ever obfuscating their legacy, their work and their passion, for without them, we would not be puffing up our feathers of achievement until much later in life, if at all.

On a personal note, I will tell you that Austin Maynard, pictured with Lourdes and me as well as Nick Groff, is a perfect example of showing respect to our founders, our community and to himself. Yes, I'm a fan! I recall my old friend parapsychologist Peter Jordan recently appearing on a podcast being interviewed, and he voiced one major reason he stepped away from the paranormal field for a while, saying (paraphrasing), "People are putting forth things as if they are new, and they're not new. I wish they would at least be familiar with the research and work that took place for years before them."

To this point, I not only agree with Peter, but I also hope this book and my previous three somehow make their way into his hands. He may differ on theories, ideas, beliefs and more from what it is I have come to present as my platform, but he would at the least realize that folks like him and the ITC pioneers who made what I do possible GET the respect, acknowledgment and praise that they deserve from my era's researchers who are making the waves to ripple onwards into the next era.

3. The Grokking Dead

Grokking

Definitions from Oxford Languages– Verb INFORMAL•US – gerund or present participle:

- understand (something) intuitively or by empathy.

Carl! – Ok, who didn't want that as the first word of the chapter...assuming you watched *The Walking Dead* on AMC and Netflix. Awesome show; I digress...

One of the most insanely cool, fascinating and bizarre experiences Lourdes, Tony and Cherie Rathman, and I experience when doing DRV and/or Staticom is when a voice from beyond, spirit or another dimension (yes, that debate of from where rages on) describes or comments on our environment and what we see around us. They, of course, are not physically present in all of their glorious corporeal form, yet they are privy and aware of the colors, shapes, actions and more that are happening right around us, right at the moment they're happening. Incredible! Without eyes, how do they possibly attain information that in its purest form of data processes through our sensory inputs such as rods and cones, etc.? One working theory we all see a lot of potential in is that the dead or spirits with whom we're interacting are grokking the information from the collective unconscious, via OUR sensory input. You see, if the theory largely put forth by the brilliant philosopher Dr. Bernardo Kastrup suggests that our consciousness is connected to the greater collective, but as he states metaphorically, individual whirlpools spawn within each of our brain transceivers and form our subjective and egoic experience. But we are also connected in the morphic resonance sense and thus continue to have input into it, which is what we are beginning to believe to be HOW spirits can accurately describe our physical environment, actions and more. It is aggregated via sensory input, but since they do not possess a physical meat suit, they pull it from the stream of collective consciousness that we all remain contributors to, as also put forth by the explanation behind the Akashic records. IT IS possible that we are literally letting them see our realm through our eyes.

Now, while it is true that proving theories like this beyond all doubt will always remain damn near impossible, like the accepted worldviews of reductionist science, it mainly takes a mob-rule, majority-belief system to make it pretty much the standard. As I continue to read, research and try to comprehend all of this paranormal stuff, I remain open to the possibility of one or more alternative explanations for how spirits can come through devices or imprint upon them, such as the case with EVP, and spot on tell us about what we can instantly verify by our own ability of sight. This may also have precedence in the sensory input of sound, imagery and emotion...all of which are detectable as energy forms or emissions.

There are like-minded ideas out there already, if you think about it. The soul inhabits the physical body and, through its sensory mechanisms, processes data, which is incorporated into consciousness. If one were to believe a fellow human being to be possessed, in the dark and evil sense of it, that consciousness or soul would be attuned to the surroundings using the same physical sensory mechanisms that they are not, as they say in the car sales world, the original owner of, at all.

Now, I am not an expert or even experienced in remote viewing, but perhaps it is a medium's way of exploring the collective unconscious to see through someone else's mechanisms from afar. Perhaps THAT is how they envision your sofa, table and chairs and placement of decorative pieces from all the way across the continent; and yes, I have experienced that. Look up Mariah Kunau. She resides in San Francisco, yet she described much of my New Jersey apartment, where she had NEVER visited or seen pictures of at that time. She nailed a lot of it remotely.

So in the spirit communication and even, perhaps, remote viewing sense, are we open to being sensory possession participants? Is it possible that the eyes are not only the gateway to the soul, as we romanticize when discussing looking into someone's essence from the outside, but also an ocular gateway to spirits to see our realm and all of its sensory input, as well? Would this not also support the "everyone has some mediumistic capabilities" argument made by some of the most renowned mediums of the present and past ages?

Varying perspectives in a variety of studies and theories about consciousness suggest that the world outside of our brains is data that we ingest via sensory input or, in part, grok without even realizing it. So it really begs the question, "How do any entities or spirits, during any audio recordings or video recordings, accurately report on shapes, colors, attendees, actions and much more regarding our visual setting?" If, in that very sterile and quantitative view, this available data that tells US all about our environment is intuited and soaked in through our physical senses, then infused into our consciousness, which is, of course, conducted through our brains in a permissive manner, how do the voices we cannot trace back to any source report back the same conclusions that we see and hear ourselves?

Always leaving room for the unknown factor since we are discussing the unknown, I would narrow down how this happens to two possibilities; again, this is categorizing via what we know and can ascertain applying that knowledge.

Either spirits, entities or the communicators responding to us can somehow access our realm visually, acquiring the same data via sensory input or consciousness that tells US what our surroundings include and thus know as well...or...they are in fact grokking that data and its values through our senses and depositing it into our consciousness...which in turn shares it via a universal collective unconscious.

The only thing that can be challenged in this theory are the words and responses themselves. Once we can vet the authenticity of them and the certainty of what we believe is being said (and I hate that I used the word "believe" here, but it flows), then we can move beyond IF these are responses, contextually placing them within this coherent dialog, and shift focus as to HOW they are able to report back despite not being corporeal and in our space to be identifiable by us, using the same sensory inputs.

We have all seen this time and time again where our environment, apparel, haircut (or lack thereof) actions and attendee numbers are ALL called out from the great beyond via our audio systems. This is more than routine most times, with ITC sessions, using a variety of methods, but of course for us, most prominently doing DRV and Staticom. I would think by now the conundrum is more than evident. We understand our physical world as being perceived through sensory input having to do with vibration, frequency and more. Rods and cones for sight, decibels and tones for hearing. Touch and all means of physical contact with regard to vibratory rates. So, then it sort of leaves us at a major loss for how a discarnate voice from wherever it is somehow speaks with startling accuracy about characteristics within our physical environment at the moment of contact.

Are they actually seeing with eyes like ours but from another realm through some sort of mystical portal or tear in the veil? Are they using technology that permits some sort of quantum tunneling into our existence, and thus they can see us like we see an NFL football game as it is happening in a city far, far away from our couches where we sit while viewing it.

Ron Yacovetti

I have spent more than a fair share of time, and seemingly more than many ghost-hunter peers, on figuring out how data or information leaves our realm more than how it comes into it. This I had come to find was a much more rare mindset than it should be. Using what we DO know about physics, accepted, quantum, etc., look at what is, in some way, taking place. Our thoughts and/or vocals are reaching somewhere unseen and soliciting responses. Read that again if it helps it to sink in. Now within ITC, our technical methods are questioned more than Al Capone on tax day, yet they produce voices that can be verified via voice print in audio software. So, let's assume that we hear "Don't go to the bar" via a ghost box and then speak those words into our software of choice and verify that those are the very words we're hearing. Now... let's assume prior to that, we asked, "Should we go to the bar to celebrate our team's victory, tonight?" – making the voice capture a response, not just words. At this point, for many, the anomaly and mystery ends. Voices from beyond came through, spoke, and they had timing and relevance. ALL of that IS true. But...it began to irk me that our standard understanding of how sound works, behaves and travels does not fully paint the picture of how anyone outside of our immediate physical space can hear us TO respond to us. Mechanical sound waves only propagate so far before the cohesiveness of the air evens and thins them out and they cease to go on. So we're left looking at quantum mechanics (QM), consciousness, zero-point energy (ZPE), wave functionality of photons (light) as well as superluminal communication, which states data would be traveling beyond the speeds of light, which, of course, sounds like sci-fi at its best.

The answer remains something that eludes us with a few possibilities amongst that list. It was the wild and more and more plausible-sounding superluminal communication idea, posited by the incredibly brilliant author and PhD in philosophy Bernardo Kastrup, that stuck in my mind and had me thinking nonstop. In essence, taking into account consciousness, morphic resonance and the idea of collective unconscious (aka mind), the only way information could be somewhere quicker than the speed of light would theoretically be if it were already there! Superluminal communication states that the spirit or mind of the human is already one with everything and everyone (not delving as far as panpsychism) with sentience, so the information asked for or desired is there in a snap because it was always there.

This would explain the EVP and ITC responses that answer our questions before or just a split second after we finish uttering them. It would push the boundaries of the materialist mindset to suggest even between people, that such transference of sound from one to another, the thought process (if only in a mechanistic sense) to aggregate the reply, then utter it, then have it heard, deciphered and understood...and all THAT fast?

I understand I am not a physicist or PhD, but I am very experienced and educated on the things that are known factors and potential factors of my spirit communication methods. I also agree wholeheartedly with the brilliant Bernardo Kastrup (*Science Ideated*) when he says that the physicist has no right to take a moral high ground and criticize the non-physicist for engaging in physical speculation, because physics today is speculating in farfetched ways that push the bounds of the human mind's potential for extremes (para-phrased). He cites multiple types of parallel universes, multi-dimensional infinity, ten spatial dimensions, the nature of time being illusory, and dark matter as examples of how much physicists are reaching out for some possible explanations for so many of the things we cannot explain.

And as a fellow philosophically minded person, though mine is more rooted in satire, I agree with Bernardo Kastrup in all of that. In fact, it is in league fully with the words of the irreproachable biologist Dr. Rupert Sheldrake when he said that there is a materialist ethos in science as cosmologists come up with things like multiple universes, billions of actual universes besides our own, for which NO EVIDENCE exists to support it all, yet it becomes totally mainstream with the accepted worldview of science. No one throwing a tantrum for its lack of a foundation, lack of evidence...no one being ridiculed or attacked over it...nothing. And he believes that it dodges those filters because it does not attempt to over-turn an ideology. He feels that what is at stake in these instances is NOT science...it's an ideology. That, I agree, is the truth and needs to be undone, if at all possible.

4. Superluminal: Faster Than the Speed of Light?!

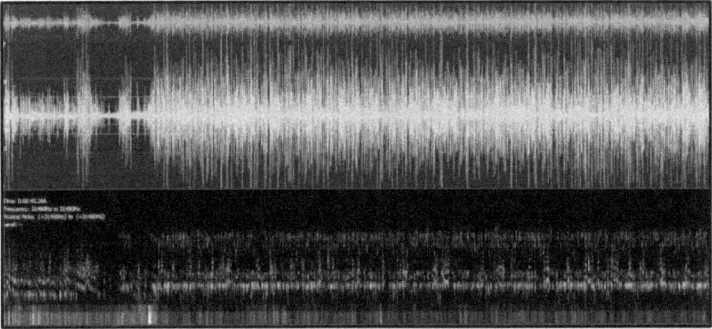

ONE OF MY favorite aspects of the paranormal field, its thinkers and the boundless possibilities since we are always operating at a deficit of wisdom and facts, is how a seemingly out-of-left-field concept can suddenly make SO much sense. It can be an epiphany moment we experience ourselves or something we learn from reading, listening or some combination of the two. In this instance, for me, in studies about consciousness by the amazing Dr. Bernardo Kastrup, I learned of a theory about consciousness that my mind connected the dots on immediately to the Staticom, DRV and

EVP work we have done for years. This is something that for context and ingenuity purposes, I try to keep myself aware of at all times: that the data and information I am gleaning from consciousness studies and research may or may not have been inclusive of any or all psychical phenomena. Why is this important? Because when referencing, citing or even foot-noting the works that led to a concept or theory, I do not want to mislead or seem to intuit more than I can justify about this all. But I do find this piecemeal mental collage assembly process fascinating, since so often that is how brilliant concepts and applications of them can be and are born. In this instance, those of us who have done EVP and ITC sessions know how quickly voices can come in. Added to that and oftentimes even more staggering is how abruptly quickly, how instantaneously these directly timed and relevant responses show up. I mention this every time I lecture, how voices will answer us so often just before or just after we complete asking a question. How is that possible? How can any intelligent being reply with a timed, relevant, calculated reply without the due time to accept, decipher, process and utter any reply at all? Do you realize how many marriages could be saved with improved communication, if the shouting from other rooms of the word "WHAT?!" were out of the equation! I comically digress...well, a little...the point is, there is an efficacy of contact that mechanical sound waves within our own environment almost never can produce! And you know what is really odd here? When people say "oh, you're such a cute couple, finishing each other's sentences," it may not only or even at all be attributed to familiarity with each other, but also to something that may very well be the smoking gun to how all anomalous vocal phenomena takes place...superluminal communication...FASTER than the speed of light!

Now, wait a minute, Mr. Yackity Yacman! There are two problems with that outlandish and bold statement from the physics side of things. First of all, says my devil's advocate, light is a constant and cannot vary as a result of being a constant...right? Well...no, not exactly...yep, it's seatbelt time again...

One thing I learned in recent years and do not think I wrote about previously, but if I did, excuse my forgetfulness, is how light works with regard to distance and time. One incredibly clear example I recall learning was how one of us could stand at the end of a mile-long road, with a car facing us at the opposite end, exactly one mile away. Assuming, for example, that it is nighttime and dark outside; the headlights of the vehicle are now on. The light that emanates from the headlights will travel towards us at precisely the same rate of speed regardless of whether or not that vehicle is racing towards us feverishly or standing completely still. No difference whatsoever.

Also something I found to be incredibly cool and beyond ironic is how St. Thomas Acquinas, a philosopher from the eighteenth century, described angelic beings and their ability to traverse distances or move about with absolutely NO loss of time across any length or distance of space, a description that today is mirrored in any quantum physics explanation of how photons of light operate and behave. How amazing is that? Beings of light, angels, and properties of light in our realm noted in vastly different eras, yet by use of the same characteristics.

One thing that is not inherently a paranormal topic, but is a favorite of Lourdes when she speaks with me on lecture events, is noting the brilliant works of Dr. Rupert Sheldrake, biologist. A former SPR member (Society for Psychical Research), Dr. Sheldrake is a crusader for the sciences being set free from the restraints, expectations and biases of materialism and scientism. He is a genuine researcher, skeptic and human being; and this is a proper use of the label skeptic because he does seek the truth and absolution, not just what he would like to believe to be true.

In his endeavors, which I encourage everyone reading this to also read, Rupert noted something incredible about the alleged constants in science: gravity, speed of light, etc. He states that the measured value of c, which is the identifier for the speed of light as a constant, HAS CHANGED or fluctuated between 1928 and 1945. He went and paid a visit to the head of Metrology of the Physics Lab in Teddington. During their discussion, behind closed doors one would have to imagine, the meteorology professor says, "c (the speed of light) cannot change, it is a constant! We explain the drop you are talking about with 'intellectual phase locking.' So now, we have now solved that problem. We fixed the speed of light by definition in 1972. It might still change, but since we define the meter from c, we would never know."

Dr. Sheldrake points this out as having also been classified as "science's biggest embarrassment" since this professor told him that the reason a constant cannot change is because, after all, it IS a constant. Now clearly, if labels from a person of science could not be overturned or rethought, Pluto would still be considered a planet, but it is not. This, Sheldrake argues, is proof of ideology and bias not a seeking of the truth; I would agree.

So, circling back to the speed of light and its possible connection to spirit communication, would such variations, which again happened in a flap of time, be possible explanations for how anomalous vocals traverse our realm and there and back? It is interesting to consider, yet may still hold a modicum of truth or perhaps explain more than my less-than-PhD mind realizes. But it is a different theory that piqued my interest in how much it appears to be in league with many aspects of DRV and Staticom spirit contact characteristics than not. Back to Dr. Bernardo Kastrup.

In his book *Science Ideated* (and I am sure in others it is mentioned), Dr. Kastrup references something within consciousness study called *superluminal communication*. Super, just like in supernatural, means beyond the natural, usual norm. So by definition this means greater than light (or its speed) in communications.

The differences from here may lie more in context and circumstance than in terminology used to posit one thing or another. It is natural for all of us to look at communication and contact as information traveling between two points or people and then factoring in time/space, sound, etc. to break out the details of how it can and does play out. But what this revolutionary idea in the framework of spirit communication suggests, in just one aspect of it, is the elimination of the time/space facet of it, regarding traversing any distance, be it vast or miniscule.

Superluminal meaning faster because it is always present as part of the collective unconscious, morphic field and Akashic records, in theory and concept. So it doesn't travel TO where we are, as it is already there and need only be revealed when called upon or asked for. Nothing transient needs to happen. Teleportation is not a necessity, as the information sought is, if such is our truth, merely hidden and not detectable to our senses and in part our devices used to capture audio-visual occurrences.

Perhaps a great metaphor and real-life example of this type of thing is the internet. I do not have any physical items, logs, books or the like that tell me what the top-rated restaurants in my ten-mile-radius area are, but, with my being dialed into this interwebs thing, I have immediate access to such information in an instant. So our homes, our lives, our individual existences are often encased within our cell phone of choice, that is tantamount to our self-reflective, egoic existence. Our personal lives within us, tributaries that are still tethered to the larger body of water, the lake or global ocean from which it branched away, yet remains a part of...so things that are inherent in its makeup and have universal characteristics can be known to all with identical properties, and then from there, within our egoic path are the qualia, metacognitive function and the sentience that we do not share with others in the same mirrored way that we absorb the color red via sensory input.

Isn't that, in and of itself, an exciting thought or realization to come to?...even as a possibility. If we look at the concept of imagined, then birthed with regard to creative works, be it physical structures, musical compositions or otherwise, then isn't the modern-day global community whose infrastructure is almost entirely the worldwide web, something that seems to be the physical manifestation of the Akashic records, morphic fields, collective unconscious theory and/or existence? If this bears truth, then that would pose a major monkey-wrench issue for the materialist idea of the brain creating what we deem to be consciousness. There would be no way for individual brains to birth our sentient selves, our consciousness and simultaneously be part of a cognitive global net that connects us all. Wouldn't that mean that ONE of the brains on the planet had to have hatched this plan in order for it to pan out in any sensible way? If it did, how would everyone else dial into it to be collectively connected? What physiological differences caused THAT person to be the father or mother of collective consciousness, and if more than one person is/was capable of being it, how did some form of natural selection determine WHO it ended up being? See how unfounded skepticisms rooted in looking to shoot holes in things no matter what can lead you down paths that you cannot explain the origins of or make a case for getting lost along it, at all, at any point once having begun.

This is an evolutionary, educational journey for me, and this brings me to where I will certainly dive deeper in chapter seven, into the study (or lack thereof) of consciousness. The more that I look at the landscape of paranormal investigating, the more I see a greater focus on ways to experience phenomena, ways to capture phenomena but much less emphasis on the role that consciousness may very well play in all of it. At this point in my research and experimentation with vocal anomalies and more, I am comfortable saying that the understanding of consciousness, as best we can, will help our critical thinking, theorizing and deducing our way closer and closer to the brass ring of knowing that absolute and elusive truth of the unknown.

In the time approaching the conclusion of this book being written, I'd heard from an old friend Bill Murphy, whom you recognize from the show *Fact or Faked*. He is, all hyperbole aside, one of the most brilliant-minded researchers not representative of any university or elite organization, just a brilliant, undaunted researcher whose work is stellar to say the least. Bill shared some experimentation and theory he'd been steeped in since last we had spoken, and it was mind-blowing in its essence AND its timing: torsion fields and coherent biofields, which are hypothetical information transfer mechanisms, according to Bill. They are also defined by Google as "...also called axion field, spin field, spinor field, and microlepton field, and is a feature of pseudoscientific proposals that the quantum spin of particles can be used to cause emanations to carry information through vacuum orders of magnitude faster than the speed of light."

Needless to say, so I shall say it anyway, because that seems to be the useless purpose of that phrase, haha, THIS definition excites me. The possibilities that may, individually or collectively fused, facilitate what to us appears to be faster-than-light-speed communication is beyond exhilarating as concepts go. Quantum-level conveyance of data or information at speeds in excess of matter transfer via photons of light is intriguing to me, for a variety of reasons, one of which I DID write about in prior books of mine. There was the investigation that Lourdes and I were invited to join, alongside Robert and Sandra Bandov of Bearfort Paranormal, Rich Moschella, and New Jersey Paranormal's John Ruggerio and Chris Therrien. In short, doing DRV, direct radio voice, under the surface of the earth inside the depths of a zinc mine, where cell phones, radios and their respective signals go to die, WE RECEIVED DIRECT VOCAL RESPONSES. Something acausal or at the least dissociated from a standard RF signal carrier wave, likely on a quantum level, allowed some anomalous vocals to enter the environment and answer us, in the most inexplicable, vetted scenario. Could ZPE (zero-point energy), torsion fields or any combination of things be the facilitator of the contact we experienced? It is theoretically possible, and thus, we continue looking into the possibility.

5. The Philip Experiment
Misused to Debunk Spirit Voices

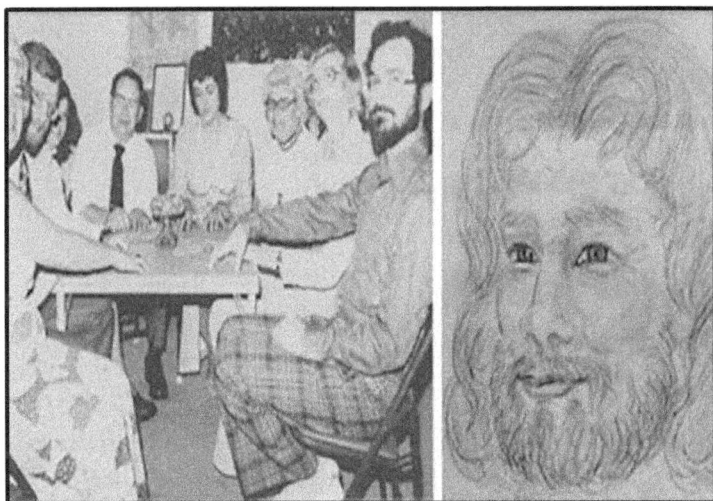

THIS IS one of those things like the hearing-test-based experiment launched online known as Laurel and Yanny that people who talk about the paranormal will oftentimes mention, usually in a quest to debunk, discredit or provide a more rational explanation for a paranormally based phenomena. I have taken a deep dive into this online mystery of hearing in my lectures as well as in my previously written books – the short version of this experiment in hearing and sound goes as follows...

A mixed rerecording was created by students who played the sound of the word "laurel" while rerecording the playback amid background noise in the room. The audio clip of the main word "laurel" originated in 2007 from a recording of a talented opera singer named Jay Aubrey Jones. Jay uttered the word "laurel" as one of a couple of thousand pronunciations produced to be a reference and published by vocabulary.com during 2007. The clip was made at Jones' home using a laptop and microphone, with acoustic foam to soundproof the recording, an attempt at sound quality made at the time, it seems.

Important to note on this – that it was not ONE message played that people heard totally different, with some hearing Yanny and others hearing Laurel – BOTH were embedded in the audio clip, but factors such as age (where high-frequency hearing loss sets in), familiarity (you know people named Laura or Laurel), and more can sway which you actually hear, should both be detectable to you. And...playing the "laurel" clip over speakers and rerecording it introduced noise and exaggerated the higher frequencies. This is the very principle by which we feel ghost boxes, direct radio voice and now Staticom function, by the use of stochastic resonance via white noise. But people who recall this, to this day, would argue that it shows how flawed we hear since one sounded-out word was repeatedly heard as two different words by many, many people. Again, appetizers, exit and post a full facility review. Take it easy, Mary!

So...where was I? Oh yes...my friend Phil...or Philip, we're not THAT close...well not yet. He is, after all, a figment and manifestation of other people's imagination, not mine.

Many times in discussions about spirit communication or contact, the concept of Tulpas and thought forms will come up. It has been mentioned along with many reported cases of paranormality, boldly including such areas of study such as ITC, instrumental transcommunication.

Now, if you consider Ouija boards or pendulums as ITC, sure...maybe it qualifies to be brought up. But to be fair, if you do consider those as ITC, you're way behind on your studies and should back up a few steps to review ITC history and take notice of the absence of such methods. Not all spirit contact is ITC, but all ITC "is" a means of spirit contact, a valiant effort if not successful, but a means of spirit contact nonetheless.

Regardless, the point of this chapter is that one cannot walk into a restaurant, have one cocktail and an appetizer, then leave, go home, and give the place a five-star review. You've barely scratched the surface of the environment, its surroundings, and how things go, yet you have the foolhardy confidence and brash mindset and speak on it as if you have taken in a whole and complete experience. We see this in the paranormal world just as audaciously as anywhere else. This experiment, which was a brilliant concept, is addressed and slung into conversations without those doing so possessing the full breadth of the experiment, its goals, successes, failures, and most of all its exclusions: things that were never a part of it, yet get tied to it in the misuses of it within conversations.

The well-known and exceptionally documented Philip Experiment, which took place in the early 1970s and was orchestrated by the Toronto Society for Psychical Research (TSPR) was launched for the sole purpose of seeing if they could create a ghost. Spirit manifestation, up until that moment, was only conceived of in the context of an existing spirit making itself known, but now there are folks of varying degrees of higher education, and they were going to DIY a ghost themselves, by golly.

Their plan, in short, was to assemble a group of people who would collaborate to create a completely fictional character and then, through séance sittings, see if they could connect with him or her and receive messages and other physical phenomena, with the brass ring being to view with their own eyes, a ghost they birthed themselves. The team was composed of some brilliant and accomplished people, ranging from the role of housewife to industrial designer, and MENSA members.

Their character, clearly named Philip, was an Englishmen from the 1600s who was a man of the Catholic faith and married to a beautiful yet cold woman, with whom he had one daughter. The story goes that, while traveling about, he came upon a gypsy woman who captivated him, and he fell in love with her instantly. He would have an affair by keeping her in a stable building near the home, until, of course, he was found out. His mistress was tried for witchcraft and executed. Philp sat idly by and said nothing to defend her in the hopes of averting the execution. This later weighed heavily on his mind, leading him to commit suicide and end his own life. That may be the best fusion of fantasy and soap opera ever penned. But that was the life story of the completely fabricated character named Philip.

The whole concept and what it set out to do is amazing, to me. They were not dismissing paranormality or mocking it but, rather, shifting the focus to the interaction between the human(s) who interpret the spiritual interactions and the source behind the other party deemed a spirit or ghost. Any result other than the empty yet loud sound of crickets, a universal audible clue for failure, would actually be a step forward in the confirmation of psychical phenomena. There are tons of studies and documented cases where psi-based phenomena are considered the root cause of a supernatural experience. Showing our minds (notice I did not say brain, as these are not synonymous) can manipulate, alter and affect matter and any perceived solid object does lend credence to a handful of claims throughout the years that were rejected, mocked, disrespected, and just shut down due to being dumb. There's that odds thing I have mentioned in at least one of my previous books, that the skeptic/cynic needs to be right one hundred percent of the time for the phenomena NOT to be possible, but the believer in it, well, they need only be right once, and the grounds for possibility has been established. This is also why ANYTHING executed in the paranormal that is of note is scrutinized in ways that seem to be as granular as possible to ridiculous in nature. The Philip Experiment more than likely drummed up such from all possible interested parties...cynics, paranormal fanatics, people steeped in religiosity and more.

The reports and data acquired and created by this project were extensive and quite well done. The short version of this is that they DID create phenomena in the moment, on demand and, for many, displayed clear-cut proof that paranormal occurrences are more than likely psi-based and the manifestation of the person or persons in attendance at the time something supernatural in nature goes down.

Now, much like I've always said of debunkery and the efforts to show how to replicate or closely mimic any act deemed to be paranormal, doing such does not debunk anything. There is, for those who don't mind being bogged down with attention to detail and accuracy, a difference between ruling out the phenomena as always being fraud or misinterpretation and showing an alternative means of creating it. If someone had shown Dorothy another way to get home, that yellow brick road would've been less magical and not the only path to the desired end result. The point being, showing a secondary way or means to get somewhere, literally or figuratively, does not quash the first known or theorized way of doing so; it just raises the awareness of other ways. So...the irony of the Philip Experiment is that in its core goal, to manifest a visualization of a ghost or spirit, it failed. This is vital, to me, on a moralistic and genuine honesty level, because most people who cite this case to refute something claimed to be evidence of the paranormal likely do not realize that their smoking gun is, for its purpose, a failure. Something to think about. Ironically, from a paranormal perspective, it did yield a lot of fascinating and undeniable phenomena that cannot be explained by having been hoaxed, misinterpreted or outright misconstrued. Those things happened, and several in attendance, participants and onlookers alike, witnessed it. THAT is pretty cool. But by the same token, sobering enough to take note of how it played out versus the desired goal. One wouldn't cite the outcome of the Hindenburg to raise capital for a new zeppelin or blimp project...you get the point.

Also, more of what is interesting to ascertain from this historic experiment is the fact that no audible evidence such as EVP (electronic voice phenomena) or anything remotely close to ITC (instrumental transcommunication) was captured or noted in any of the coverage and data available about the experiment. Why is this important? Hmm...how much time do you have? Ha! I'll explain...

Many times, those of us who spend our time and money on audible paranormal phenomena are told by the doubters, cynics and sometimes simply unaware that our thoughts are projected out and onto the tape recorders, digital recorders and, most odd of all, through the barren longwave radio frequency of a world band radio in use during DRV, direct radio voice. From my knowledge, and please write to me and update me if I missed anything, there is no data to suggest that a human being's thoughts can be sent airborne, then fused in the moment with the carrier wave of a longwave AM frequency band. This whole concept I've talked about in books and lectures before and make mention of the can of worms opened when introducing this argument for anomalous voices. Remember, I am the continuity-of-thought guy, so you cannot say that such an outside of the normal action is doable without first thinking through what limits it has, may have and would not have, in all imaginable instances.

For a prime example, which I know I've written about before, if one can, in fact, project their thoughts out into the room and fuse them with the radio waves into and/or out of the radio on a vacant channel, how does the process determine whom in a room full of attendees to bring in vocally and whom to exclude? How is it determined to bring in the one voice at a time and not the many at once, mashed up like some sort of audio mulch and compost collection? Are any such instances inclusive of a territory accent or a dialect indicative of where the audio experience took place? And, as many pioneers of EVP and ITC in Europe have noted historically, how do these people suddenly think and project out languages, sense of humor, jargon, proprietary information and more when none of it was ever consciously known to them, at all? How many known and then researched cases are there where one's inner thoughts, perhaps griping about having to go back to work on a Monday, have leaked out from the cavernous microscopic realm of our brains to the macroscopic world of cars and their very full-sounding radios? I know of none – but remember – I always make it a point to say that any research that seems to have a vital role in a given subject may or may not exist, but I myself do not know about it. I am always open to and aware of the idea I could be incorrect about anything...well, most things...a few things...see why I ended up divorced? Ha. My ex and I are good friends – I jest and digress once more...

Overall, with regard to the Philip Experiment, there was NO audio capture of an anomalous nature – none – and they did have video cameras running, so one would assume that possible means of catching a voice from beyond did exist for those involved. But I'll get to the cameras soon enough because it is, for me, the most difficult thing to wrap my head around with the experiment. I am not aware of voice recorders themselves having been used; none that I can find noted. And of course, this is before the golden age of cell phones that can record audio and video at a moment's notice, so planning to capture sound, in anticipation of possible EVPs, especially of the manmade manifestation variety, I would think would've been in place. So for the moment, using the Philip Experiment to refute paranormal audio because "See? We can create that stuff ourselves, in the moment, and record it" has NO basis and no support from good ole Phil.

Now, here is where I look at the big picture, and my head begins to swell with a chemical blend of confusion, oversight, absurdity and WTF (go ahead and look this last acronym up if necessary. I'll wait).

The cameras...

Of course, when gathering in front of around fifty people in a large room to do a brilliantly themed dark seance-like experiment, quality cameras are employed and recording every bit of the event from start to finish. This part IS true. However... and you had to know now that a "however" was coming next...there was, to me, a major-league flaw in this element of the event planning that today would've made the whole instance more impactful, more compelling, and rely less on "belief" in the story told of that event years later. So...

The point that I often emphasize repeatedly at lectures, on podcasts and more is that we are all human beings, fallible and biased by nature, above all else. So if you hold a PHD, a master's, a membership card for MENSA and any of a variety of engineering degrees, that attainment exists in your self-identity below humanity: being a human being. Seems to me, to make the most sense to take the broader concept and then what follows as within it. See, reductionists? I buy into your mantra a wee bit.

Even if the IR/night-vision lights were not commercially available. Even if any business looking for such security camera systems would've been forced to spend thousands of dollars, putting it out of a reasonable price range for folks doing an experiment like Philip, assuming their budget, if any, would not have supported this, there remains one "white elephant" of a question? **Why would you prioritize mood lighting of a seance if your experiment might yield extraordinary results you would not be able to successfully record in the dark?!**

This should call into question ANY MENSA membership for missing that or making that choice knowingly. Either prepare to record the event as it shall unfold, OR for crying out loud, turn on the lights, team genius! Go ahead back to chapter one when that uppity survey made having a degree and university a must for accuracy and reliability. Mensa and some PhDs couldn't figure out how to plan to capture phenomena in low light in 1972?

We know for certain that night-vision cameras were in use starting from 1939. The typical release of cutting-edge tech in America may also be a thing in this instance, whereas when a new technology comes out, it is insanely expensive once made commercially available, then years later becomes a digestible cost for the average citizen. That's fine. But you are conducting an experiment meant to demonstrate psychical phenomena. Don't you think that MAYBE...maybe... someone else, others, anyone not present might want to see this event, review this event, and perhaps use it as precedent in support or subverting other phenomena testimonials? Again, "Go, Team Genius!" I am beyond compelled in these situations to permit my skepticism and satirical mindset to have a field day with this stuff because it seems to me, in such an instance, that elite-level PhDs and academic experience did nothing to help at all. A DIY expert would have more likely figured out, via sense of purpose, what was at stake and how to ensure it gets recorded. So...for those keeping score, that's another point for Team Ghosthunter.

6. The Hypocrisy of Temporized Telegraphy

How a Single Technique Has Been Wielded to Prove and Disprove the Existence of Spirits and Ghosts

te leg ra phy

Definition from Oxford Languages: Noun

- *Telegraphy is the long-distance transmission of messages where the sender uses symbolic codes, known to the recipient, rather than a physical exchange of an object bearing the message.*

So this is a fun chapter for me because it has an element to it that I have had a passion for since I was a young lad. Yes, a grown man from New Jersey used the word lad. It works, I think. Anyway...

I have always been fueled by what my ex-wife, Julie Falcon-Mackie (now remarried and a fantastic mother), would refer to as a "gotcha moment." I admit it; I love spotlighting hypocrisy and any lack of continuity of thought when I see it. It was not born of my years as a satirist, aka stand-up comedian, it was a big reason why I became one. Where, you may now be wondering, is the continuity-of-thought or hypocrite issue with telegraphy? Is it related to the eventual admission of hoaxing that was later recanted by the Fox sisters? No, not at all, but it is related to them, and I'll explain why that is.

First, for those who may not know, that is technically what their form of communication using rappings, tappings and knockings is considered. Like a telegraph, and as noted at the onset of the chapter, it uses symbolic codes known to the recipient. The Fox sisters, as well as others of their time, used this method to display and declare communication with the spirit world. Oftentimes, simple yes and no questions would be asked, using one knock for a yes response and two knocks for a no.

More elaborate versions of this technique played out would include a similarity to the infamous and often feared Ouija board, where the message exchange involves spelling each word in response to what has been asked by the human beings conducting the sitting or by the spirits who are initiating a message of great importance. Either way, this is one of the earliest known versions of telegraphy.

Modern versions of this have surfaced in a variety of forms, from an electronic electromagnetic-sensor-based Ouija board with lights, to the numbers of knocks meant to indicate letters in the alphabet based on how many knocks come in, in succession. This last means of using telegraphy is being displayed nationally by the very cool and gifted "Paranormal Couple," Cody DesBiens and Satori Hawes, daughter of ghost hunter of excellence Jason Hawes.

In previous books of mine, I have made it a point to mention them and the use of telegraphy for two main reasons. One of the reasons being that the form of this type of communication with the spirit realm may actually be new and unknown to many of today's generations. The fact that these two are bringing it back, and with a charismatic flare and romanticized appeal, is freaking awesome! It is an old technique resurrected by newer participants within paranormal research, and that is how the greatest from those before us get carried forward with an element of respect just by doing it. The other reason is the same reason almost; with number two being that because it IS an older means, it is important that we not imply a founding and pioneering of the method versus a bringing-it-back vibe. To fail to do so would be to erase the labors of those who launched the modern spiritual movement. Cody and Satori are wonderful people who will be influencing the generations to follow, much like Satori's dad, Jason Hawes, did whilst not even realizing it at the time. I love this...for one thing, because I myself live it.

Anyone who knows ANY of my work knows that I have incessantly given credit and shown reverence for the ITC greats who came before me and without whom I may never have been on the path in life that I have come to embrace and enjoy so much. I have been somewhat scolded by Anthony Simonelli and Johnny Zaffis for not taking more credit for myself and the developments in ITC, DRV and now Staticom than I do, versus crediting those from the past much more than myself. It's a habit of mine since I am acutely aware that I would not be doing what I am doing, loving and prospering educationally on it, if not for their work and the shot on the chin they took to make it known at a time it was supremely shunned, mocked and discredited.

Where I find the temporalization of telegraphy a bit disturbing is how cynics will cast doubts, judgments and accusations of hoaxing towards genuine spiritualist communicators like the paranormal couple, and they'll sometimes cite the aforementioned Philip Experiment as evidence that they are not communicating with spirits, because the mind created a spirit, Philip. So it's not ghosts, it's us...people. So, we're manifesting a spirit contact experience? Isn't that, in and of itself, a psychical phenomena unfolding, should it be true? Tulpa creation through repeated intentional contact with a spirit that may never have existed is another suggested explanation when such happens. When people hear that a lady hanged herself over and over, born of folklore and never shown to have any historical truth to it, they retell it, they investigate and keep asking for the spirit of this lady to come through, so some proponents of the paranormal will suggest that the spirit has been birthed at the site via psychical repetitive intention. I am still very much on the fence with this one. It leaves a lot of unexplored avenues and equally, if not more so, likely explanations very much in play, in my opinion.

Hang on a moment now...to suggest that because yes and no responses using methods rooted in telegraphy during the Philip Experiment took place via collective intent of the group, or so they concluded, means that ghosts do not exist would require the data to show the difference between spirits or ghosts utilizing the methodology and collective and morphic resonance or consciousness of the group in attendance. This all assumes, of course, that the timing and relevance of any responses with taps and raps are convincing enough to be comfortably ruled as responses and beyond the realm of coincidence.

Once that is determined, which it seems it was, then you need to either state the speculative nature of the assessment being ghosts are responding or the consciousness of those participating are behind it all. To just take one of those sides and run with it without addressing the equally possible alternative is careless and, to me, rests on the expected support of those who are members of one's like-minded camp. A major reason you may not, nor perhaps ever, see such data surface is because it is VERY difficult to delineate and, to the degree no doubt remains, may crest upon the impossible.

And in no uncertain terms am I suggesting this differentiating between voices of spirit and thoughts of the group of participants is easy. But unless your conclusion allows for both yet noting a side you are leaning towards, then you cannot declare with certainty without being able to illustrate WHY that is...and honestly, you may be totally wrong or right...but you should be able to substantiate and show why you believe whichever one you do. That's not unreasonable, to me. So with the Paranormal Couple and the Fox sisters, telegraphy, one can argue, sufficiently supports the realism of spirit communication, but when good ole Philp was conjured up and rap star took on a whole new meaning, it was telegraphy that was given as the reason ghosts or spirits DO NOT exist, that it's just us folks doing it to ourselves. Who would've thought that spirits or entities or ghosts would be the ethereal equivalent to a Swiss Army knife; an oscillating multi-tool that will fix whatever spiritual explanation you need so it fits JUST RIGHT...or perhaps more fair to be said, JUST RIGHT NOW.

7. Consciously Ignoring Consciousness?!

IN VARIOUS BRANCHES OF SCIENCE, there is a daunting question that poses a challenge to solve it, seemingly reserved for the extremely worthy, akin to Excalibur being embedded in the stone until the suitable chosen one arrives to yank it out with the thrust of a suburbanite trying to start an old lawnmower. The enigmatic ask is most famously known in academia and the sciences as "the hard problem of consciousness." This is something beyond complex and challenging to all who ponder it. The brilliant mind of philosopher David Chalmers posited this profound topic. According to Wikipedia.com, the hard problem is defined as...

> "The hard problem of consciousness asks why and how humans have qualia or phenomenal experiences. This is in contrast to the 'easy problems' of explaining the physical systems that give humans and other animals the ability to discriminate, integrate information, and so forth. Such problems are called easy because all that is required for their solution is to specify the mechanisms that perform such functions. Philosopher David Chalmers argues that even if we have solved all easy problems about the brain and experience, the hard problem will still persist."

Now before I dive into this, because I DO feel it is of the utmost importance for anyone who labels themself a student of the paranormal, I want to address what I like to call "the hardest problem of consciousness"...which is the fact that despite how pretty much ALL ghost hunters and paranormal researchers say they believe our soul is our consciousness and that it persists beyond physical death, YET it seems as if almost NO ONE or very few people are studying consciousness itself! Our entire field and our beliefs are built upon the concept of continuation of consciousness, YET it never comes up in discussions or in most books about ghosts, ghost hunting and the like. THIS, I find mildly insane and something that is imperative to change.

I let this sink in when I myself came to this realization. Now, in no way do I think I am ahead of any curve. I allow my research goals, meant to improve my vocal experiments, understand how acts of spirit may or may not work, what the worldview of science does and does not comprehend, etc., to direct my educational pursuits and what it is I spend my time reading. When I got sucked into consciousness and the varying concepts and theories about it, I found a few brilliant authors such as Dr Charles Tart, Bernardo Kastrup, Alex Tsakiris and more. And whilst none of their works spoke wholly to spirit communication, if at all, I was able to do what I always did when I learn new ideas: find if, how, and in what ways this theory plugs into the work I am doing...or not. These studies and points about consciousness and the materialist view of it with self-applied blinders began to resonate with me on a few fronts.

Then, in looking at it all in a broad sense, I came to realize some of what may be more puzzling about consciousness theory than about consciousness itself.

The concept that reality as we experience it, as we live it, is shaped or influenced by the observing of a world not only suggests that we could be forging our own individual subjective reality, but that there must then, by default, be a state of existence of the world PRIOR to being observed. So, here is where it gets philosophically deep and complex. If a state exists that is promptly and instantly affected and altered by the observation of an individual, then does that not make that unobserved state, by definition, illusory, as it is never able to be viewed. Now, if that is the case, does that not also make that state less than scientific and pretty much unfounded, because we cannot know anything about it, we cannot observe it, assess it, falsify it or any aspects of it, etc. because it is indefinitely elusive?

I also find that this is very suggestive of an anti-materialist perception of consciousness, since it seems to suggest that the brain could not be creating consciousness and reality given the idea that there exists, by this theory, a state that the brain and mind never get to experience. How could it be biologically possible for the byproduct of neural systems and synapses, in forging a self-egoic existence or state, to never be engaged by, experienced by, or at all affected by the very thing allegedly creating it...the brain. Not even the incredibly brilliant concept of filter hypothesis by Bernardo Kastrup can make that whole idea work. In order for the brain as a filter of mind and collective unconscious, tantamount to a radio receiver taking in data at a tuned frequency, to have any access to this illusory state of unaffected probability, it would have to, on some level, experience, affect or metacognitively be aware of it. It is not the case.

Now, there is another highly debated scientific topic, whether or not the brain creates or births consciousness, so by design it would have to be purely mechanistic – think of a metaphorical car in contrast to horses (i.e., by Rupert Sheldrake). Horses are sentient beings. Cars, as we all know, unless you're a *Knight Rider*, David Hasselhoff fan, or perhaps Lightning McQueen from Disney's *Cars* movie, are not. Both horses and cars go where directed. The difference is that horses may have their own desires or ideas...and more than likely do. So think about that. If the brain created consciousness and all reality, what exactly would direct IT? That concept embraced by the materialist perspective says unequivocally that the brain and directives to the body is a mechanistic design at work. So...could consciousness fall into that modality? In my opinion...and that is what I am sharing here...not at all – instead it suggests that it must be outside of the brain, as thought of when using the term "mind," in a universal, morphic resonance, Akashic field sort of way.

So if you look at the variety of techniques used, evidence of paranormality captured (alleged and compelling alike), and especially with regard to spirit communication, how do you not delve into the study of consciousness?

One of the various theories on it may plug into your work, your ideas of how it all plays out, and thus lead you to a personal and perhaps broader breakthrough. Yet much to my realization of shock, almost no one or very, very few of the ghost hunters study this subject. Just seeing the possibilities posited is exciting. Then, should you correlate any of it to how you do your sessions and evidence you've collected, it is very rewarding; not to mention a proper impetus for the educational needs, like medical practitioners, that we should also be held to a standard of, be it by ourselves or a governing body, to always stay current and continue our aggregation of theory, practice and outcome. It's called CME, Continuing Medical Education. I made reference to this in my first book, *Paranormal Speaking: Knowingly Talking to the Unknown*, because I found that concept a viable and very sensible practice to uphold within a field where developments and research are ongoing and making strikes consistently enough to make it critical to be up to speed.

This CME concept as well as the aforementioned chapters noting lack of reverence and awareness of those who came before us and this newly cited lack of study in consciousness makes the clamoring to be on TV, speaking at expos or cons and even prematurely guesting on podcasts very alarming to see. Someone with no idea who Dr. Ernst Senkowski is, whilst investigating haunted locations maybe as long as two years and armed with a commercial-grade spirit box, will step out onto the podcast platforms made available and pontificate at levels of confidence and certainty that have less foundational support than a mud hut. Now when I preach a highly encouraged, slightly less than mandated educational system in the paranormal field, I do not mean to carry over and impart to the field those same ways that public schools have sometimes put cookie-cutter, generic materials out to students that are taught as gospel. I think what came before, how it came to be, how it was done, and how it translates to this day, etc. is all valuable to teach. Let them question it all based on what may have been learned since then. Let them test it in new scenarios. Let them approach it from new angles and even reject some or all of it in light of empirical findings of their own, of course carried out with comparable controls in place.

The point being knowing how you got where you are when you did not pioneer this idea or method from obscurity. There is a priceless lesson in all of this that connects directly to what happened with Lourdes and me, Tony and Cherie Rathman, Staticom and DRV.

As I've written in previous chapters of prior books, we were the first to slow down live white noise (which if anyone else tried this sooner, it is not known, as we did look into this). If not for my being acutely aware of what the pioneers before me did, thought, and said, the breakthroughs we've had as a result of slowing it down as well as the quality of evidence would not likely even exist now. I was doing a routine thing that paranormal people do with audio evidence...slowing it down to understand, but...it was my mental recollection of the words of EVP and DRV pioneer Konstantin Raudive, where he had said the voices of spirit not only come in faster than a human can hear them, they come in faster than the vocal tract of a human is capable of uttering them. Now this is what made me venture into the idea of slowing down ALL white noise on DRV sessions, and doing it in real time to achieve what yet another pioneer had said before my time, that ITC was meant to be dialog in real time as compared to EVP, which is record and review later. Point and case made on the educational importance and it being ongoing, I think. Well, I certainly hope. The main thing we believe continues, so...ya know...maybe we should look into it a bit more.

According to Mike McRae of Science Alert (2023):

> "*Problems that are easy include integrating information into cognitive systems, or working out how we focus attention. Meaty, mechanical, physical mysteries that aren't simple to solve, but are at least straight-forward to define.*
>
> "*Hard problems are more philosophical. Like, how does a network of neurons generate the experience of smelling cut grass on a warm summer's day? How does our brain turn*

wavelengths of electromagnetism triggering reactions in your eyes into a dazzling rainbow? And how does it produce a sense of self-awareness?

"The challenge is using tools of science – such as experimentation, replication, and reasoning – to relate objective measures of cells and chemistry to subjective accounts of agency and awareness."

So...while I understand that some of the most intellectual minds of our time, such as Dr. Robert Lanza, will state convincingly that (paraphrasing this brilliant man)..."*despite how everything thought by anyone in science is processed via consciousness, we collectively know almost nothing about consciousness itself*," I still find it more bewildering that more paranormal investigator types are not studying the subject in excess. There is a wealth of knowledge available in a variety of books by philosophers, biologists, psychologists, parapsychologists and more...so read them, go with the ones that via author, book cover art, whatever...call to you and at least attain what can be obtained about the subject; then when you correlate it with your own research or experience and find theories you believe, they'll be as educated as possible. You may even find that ideas and concepts you once bought into as probable are suddenly much more or less supported by how you view your own beliefs.

It is continually showing me, through every paranormal-based discussion, event and debate, that consciousness must be as familiar to us as the most popular fad-like methods such as today's "Estes experiment." The brain itself and its role as a sort of trickster is a very commonly applied scapegoat for what we feel is phenomenal, thus labeled as brain birthed and, instead, as an epiphenomenon.

Once again, I love the words and work of Dr. Bernardo Kastrup when he points out the phenomena of "emergence" and how it is relatable to consciousness. A wizard of the metaphor, Dr. Kastrup eloquently explains that, as an example, sand dunes are a phenomena of sand and wind. Beautifully unexpected patterns are formed through this air-driven, granular process. The end results are creations that look to be intentionally and even artfully designed. But how? The great philosophers of our time call this "weak emergence" because while it is surprising compared to its components, it IS explainable by them! The properties of what you see in the dunes are attainable from its components, again being grains of sand and wind. Bernardo also points out that these design-like patterns can also be mimicked on a computer. This all, he explains, differs when the term emergence is applied to the phenomena of consciousness, as it cannot be deduced from the properties of its components. Consciousness cannot be deduced from the mass, spin and momentum of subatomic particles, he continues, and that is a major difference not to be overlooked. Now for many of us who are not at a doctorate level in philosophy (though some of us have studied it a good amount), Mr. Kastrup always gives easily digestible yet equally impactful metaphoric grounds to support such statements.

The depth of the color blue, the redness of a red tone, the pain felt emotionally at the core of our being when we lose a family member, pet or friend – these are all not phenomena that can be deduced in the reductionist-minded way, looking at momentum, mass, spin and charge. This type of phenomenon, elusive to the materialistic explanation, is what philosophers such as Dr. Kastrup or David Chalmers refer to as "strong emergence." This type of emergent phenomenology, they explain, is not coherent, where they then go on to label it an appeal to the unknown or, as Dr. Kastrup has dubbed it, as "...an appeal to magic." This brings me back to a quote in one of my earlier books by Arthur C. Clarke, which says, "Any sufficiently advanced technology is indistinguishable from magic." Now, as someone who is a practitioner of metaphysics, communication and with a contemporary technical spin, I am seeing the truth in this quote more and more. After all, people who love, hate, doubt, believe and wonder at magicians almost all believe in its being illusory and manmade, not actual acts that exist beyond the accepted worldview of science. Does that not explain a position that ITC finds itself in consistently? I believe it does.

8. Shifting the Debate: Belief in Consciousness vs. Ghosts

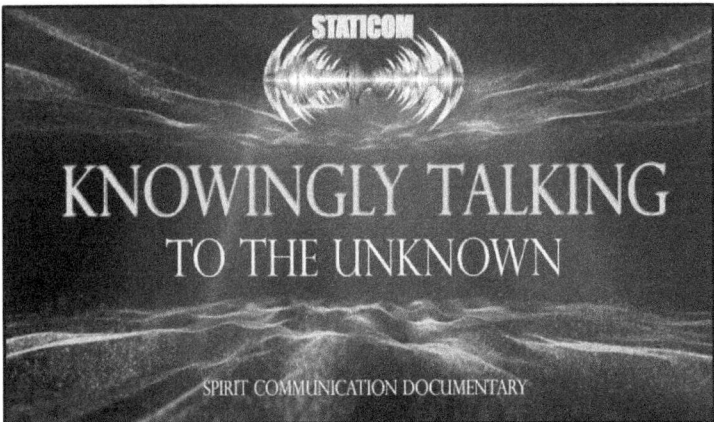

ONE OF THE biggest hurdles we face is the never-ending argument about whether or not ghosts are real. Where is the proof of ghosts? Where is the science behind it?...as well as additional questions of the same nature. One immediate setback in testifying to the legitimacy of ghosts and spirits is the social and anthropological side effects. Both of these words, especially ghosts, have acquired either negative, cartoonish or whimsical associations, which pushes the area of study away from any appearance of being scientifically done and legit, like a tissue in a hurricane. And if you connect the dots and follow the logic in and out of scientific circles, you come to realize that the ghost or spirit is what we believe to continue after physical death. We also commonly refer to things, such as our soul, more and more often nowadays, by the appropriate term, consciousness. So, syllogistically speaking, the "ghosts are real" argument is essentially and simultaneously the "consciousness is real" argument.

From a debate standpoint, this is already a small step forward because it progresses the discussion to the David Chalmers zone and the defining and framing of consciousness...a notable step because it presupposes, in the continuing dialog, that it is real, it is legit, and its nature and genesis is the REAL mystery.

Most ghost-hunter folks will get mired deep within the wrong debate and, in turn, get supremely heated up by the argument with the cynic who flies the skeptic banner (yes, in error, they are also believers, not skeptics), because they end up trying to prove and convince others based on evidence that no bias-driven cynic is ever going to accept as real. Sports teams do it, courts and legal teams do it...it's placing the debate, the topic on trial, in a fair or neutral arena, and if not that, at the least, an accurate and fair environment. The "ghosts and poltergeists and bigfoot and Loch Ness monsters and more" argument has been tainted by entertainment and bush-league investigating to the extent that they have lost credibility, and the argumentative ROI fuel is almost all but diminished. It's linguistic. It's strategic, and it is FAIR; reframe the discussion devoid of buzz words, negatively connotative words, and aligned with jargon and terminology, vernacular that is more aligned with terms of science, philosophy and reason. None of this is to suggest manipulating or molding the debate into something it is not, or conflating it at all. These are just moves that anyone making their "case" in any court, be it public, private or personal, would use in order to impress upon the key factors with language that serves the purpose not those prosecuting it. And this is really the core of what we pursue evidence of, ALL OF THE TIME. To avoid this is to ask someone to go to the store and buy you a piece of furniture. Then, when they return with a table, you say, "No, you idiot. I wanted a couch for the living room!" Did they do exactly as you'd asked? YES – Did you get exactly what you wanted? Yes and no. So, we can look at a variety of things we classify as paranormal evidence, but unless we're talking data storage in the form of a residual haunting, and IF we are talking any interactive communication or contact, then we are looking at intelligence and its unfolding in front of us... something that consciousness would sum up quite well.

Another word-related, connotative problem is that the term ghost has been lampooned, cartooned and buffooned to the point of matching the credibility devaluing that mediums received from TV infomercial psychics such as the beloved TV actress Miss Cleo. And if ghosts or spirits DO exist, as many believe (and tons of data suggests), those of the intelligent variety are essentially consciousness. Strikingly, and this is a whole other conversation and debate, what are considered residual hauntings would be much more distanced from intelligent hauntings, being little more than sensory input such as hot or cold sensations, which convey such but do not communicate it to us in any linguistic or telegraphic means. This is tantamount to looking at the color red and listening to a song in the car. Residual would be akin to pure sensory input, which consciousness would process within its range of filtration. Intelligence, different story...

Again I turn to the brilliant philosophy of Dr. Bernardo Kastrup in his saying that in relation to physical sciences and medicine and more, that doctors can and do sustain our lives, but it is in one's philosophy where it finds meaning, purpose and definition. What we live for, as he suggests, is philosophical. I agree. Our paranormal lives, both individually and as a collective, need to know their philosophical positions, or we lack the backbone to support, explain and bolster the beliefs in all else that we speak to on a regular basis.

In his book *Meaning in Absurdity*, Dr. Kastrup notes a situation where someone approaches him about the idea of consciousness continuing and says, "How can you suggest that? People are dying all around, all the time. Do you not see that?" His answer is of titanic depths when he retorts, "Did you ever notice that only OTHER people die, not you?" This is exceedingly thought provoking and, for many of us, requires it be read over and over to contemplate its profound implication. In other words, it took me a minute too...but wow, what a concept and viewpoint to hold! This is yet more proof to me that the nexus of change between what IS and what we would like it to be, for the paranormally minded, is rooted heavily in philosophy and how it is conveyed.

We are told ghosts and spirits and all of this stuff does not exist. This becomes a fool's game to argue with data that the cynic won't accept, couched in ideas they won't accept, and laid out with supporting testimony and more that...say it with me..."They won't accept." This is where I look to have a philosophy and not impedance of a circuit or the transducing of anything. To say something does not exist is to acknowledge it, which is to call it into context, which is to give it validity and thus it exists (in my own words). As Dr. Kastrup suggests in more than one of his brilliant books, "To choose good behavior is to reject bad behavior," so when someone calls out this paranormal stuff is all illusory or in their extreme layman's terms, bullshit, then I look to this perspective, as I always have with critics of movies: you cannot be a critic of a film not ever made. Your judgment or opinion of alleged data pointing to spiritual stuff is in and of itself a validation that there IS data to assess, and now we slide back to the platform of logic, bias, axioms and belief systems. And what I really like here is that this moves the discussion along, most times, to causality, and that is where the onus of proof lies equally upon the proponent of paranormality and the doubter who thinks we live in a conveniently mechanistic world. The more you read this book, I would hope, the more you realize how irrational our world actually is; and this, to quote the brilliant Mr. Kastrup, is not to imply foolishness, but rather a transcendence of logic and its limits. A bold case to support that notion that brain and body are in consciousness, NOT consciousness in the brain and outside of the body.

He refers to it as the only carrier of reality that we may know with any certainty. This, he continues, is a reason it can be very difficult to put a concrete explanation OF consciousness, as we recognize it, into mundane language.

Once you look at consciousness and the relationship with body and brain from this perspective, you see how much more there is to all of this and how it may speak in support of the realism of OUR para-absurdity. Bernardo Kastrup likens our localized reality to a whirlpool within a stream, which he thus likens to mind or consciousness. In his other masterful book *Brief Peeks Beyond,* he posits that "For the same reason that a whirlpool doesn't generate water, the body brain system doesn't generate consciousness." He counters the arguments that our brain and its neural firings are the makings and birthing of thoughts, emotions and perceptions, saying that instead, they are the observed state of those things when looked upon by someone else. Lightning, he says, is the observed state of atmospheric discharge, NOT the cause of it.

Now why is this all important to any of us paranormalists or ghost hunters or afterlife researchers? This is all consciousness and philosophy fodder. Right? At one point, I myself may have seen it that way. We go in, we talk to ghosts, we record them, we leave. Ta-dah! Proof! – yep, we all start somewhere. But now, if you look at what I've been making a case for since this chapter began, you see where this content and data is extremely important and likely useful to us all. As a whole, if we do not evolve the argument, if we do not introduce new data within new frameworks of thought, how do we expect to make any impact? Our cynics and closed-minded folks are still in their houses of brick, and we're just trying to blow them away like we did the people who are SO on board with paranormality that they're foundational beliefs are the veritable straw-and-stick-made variety.

We need to be done with arguing if ghosts are real or not. That is way too broad a topic in a word, and there is too much that goes into the discussion to simplify it that way; not to mention that it has been played out, dismissed and lost value from a stalemate between believers and doubters. This debate has, in and of itself, taken on an identity and lives on as a state of being for the question of a lifetime...do we live beyond physical death? This is why I began to push more towards learning and studying ideas, theories and concepts about consciousness and how it may work.

This has become increasingly vital to me because it not only shifts the argument to where it genuinely belongs, but also more accurately labels and identifies it, giving those who have always been believers in ghosts an area of study within which support for their cause may be found. This has been the case for me. To argue purely along the lines of what we (society) deem laws of sound would be to enter into the arena of the cynic and their circular logic. Inherent in this debate would be the given assumption and presupposition that these laws of sound govern audio phenomena, which would be odd because those laws and their proponents cannot fully explain these things, which is why they become the topic of debate and labeled justly to be phenomena.

Anyone who is at the front lines of speaking, lecturing and professing the truths of paranormality and ghosts should come to be familiar with this internal paradigm defining shift in thought. It is a weapon of mass information destruction the hardcore cynics (who call themselves skeptics) use, especially the atheistic, science-is-my-religion type. Circular reasoning is their thing. As Bernardo Kastrup points out with the arguments of materialists, which many if not all of these para-skeptics are, their criticisms are fallacious; he points out how that "beg the question," which cleverly takes the conclusion of an argument (which is their expected/desired conclusion) and plays it as the premise of the argument. Once again, his mastery of metaphors leaves me feeling as if that is how I should break it down here, for you. Mr. Kastrup says a great example of this circular reasoning would be if someone says, "God exists because the Bible says so" and "the Bible is true because it was written BY God" – which begs the question of God's existence.

This is their argument's foundation against consciousness – and best believe that it will gain support and a cult-like following more and more if we take away from them the "ghosts are real or not" debate.

They'll begin to argue that consciousness cannot encompass the body and brain because it must be generated or forged by something or someone, an entity. This is, again, circular reasoning because it presupposes that an entity must create consciousness, which is totally on par with materialism, seeing it as a wholly neural creation rather than what to me makes more sense, which is that consciousness simply is what is. Those steadfast doubters won't accept that because they will see it as needing to be reducible to complex marshaling. It is, as Bernardo states, no more difficult than saying the laws of physics create the world as we know it, and as a matter of fact, he continues, even less problematic because it does not leave us hung on that "hard problem of consciousness."

This is something that as I learn from those such as Bernardo Kastrup, Rupert Sheldrake and more, I will share and promote because I don't know if we make the impact or shift enough to even dent, let along shift, any paradigm if we do not shift and dent the argument itself from our side; think along the lines of a master sculptor. We shape it, present it, and it may exist in halls of recognition like museums of art, there for the future generations to see and marvel at what it is we had to take on to move forward with openness of thought.

9. Bye-Bye Bias: Research Has No Place for You

IT IS, for all of us probably, always somewhat of a tough pill to swallow when anyone serves up even a modicum of criticism or feedback beyond "Oh my stars, that is brilliant!" (Oh my stars, an old cartoon reference.) We all want the kudos, acknowledgment, praise and credit for the work we do in the paranormal field, especially since THAT is often all or most of any compensation we get, the true ROI (return on investment) for our time spent working on things. But if one wishes to live AS an adult within an adult world, it can not only be cruel, it can be, well...honest. And sometimes, honestly speaking, what we do is great work but has points to it that others can see some improvement within. Now, this is where that phrase most of us learned from our parents comes in..."Take from where it comes" – meaning if the person hates you, resents your work or the field, it is likely of little to no value. But if the person is a respected colleague, then that can be priceless feedback because they are not gunning down your credibility, they're giving you the most genuine commentary that they can.

Awareness of bias and the platform upon which one speaks to your work is important to know because the paranormal field is a very short cry from being like (and via television also overlaps with) Hollywood. Rejection is a common thing when in the world of glitz, glamor and waiters who have the next cinematic summer blockbuster in their car's backseat. And yes, I can speak to this with certainty, as I lived in Los Angeles for exactly fourteen years, initiated by a few VERY close calls with regard to selling feature film scripts. Killing with kindness may be the most chronic crime in LA. Coping skills, managed expectations, and the will of a bull in an arena after it sees red is the skill set necessary to brave this city beyond the moving-there, honeymoon phase. Trust me, I know. But what happens when in Hollywood or especially in the field of the paranormal, we get hit with a less than stellar review?

We all know by now that we live in the age of "reviews." Years ago, one was a critic, like in the movie industry or food and restaurant business, where people would look to them to help form or pretty much adopt their own opinions. Today, every business you can imagine is on a website where feedback and comments can be had, and that information sure can be helpful...well, if, of course, as I just mentioned here, you are aware of ANY presence of ANY bias whatsoever. Otherwise, it would be like asking a cat, assuming one could talk, how they like being dropped into a tub of water or sprayed in the face with water. Most, if not all, wouldn't utter a happy-toned response.

Bias, especially in the paranormal world, can sometimes be difficult to detect. It may be coated in compliments or a false presentation of an open mind. But sometimes it is so purposeful and its vocabulary-based vehicle is so immediate that there is either no effort or no awareness that it is as blatant as it gets.

I have had conversations as recently as yesterday where someone said to me, "If everyone who dies continues as a ghost, they would have to be all around us, and I am over fifty and haven't even had as few as five ghostly interactions." Now this same person, months prior, captured an object moving on its own, on the kitchen counter, in the middle of the night. Nothing visibly caused it to jolt or move. NOTHING. And when we looked at all possibilities at that time, such as a film of water beneath it causing it to hydroplane perhaps, what ended up the most likely was that it was an anomaly; it moved of its own volition and with no detectable influence. Yet this person who claims to never have had any paranormal or ghost experience was not at all entertaining that as a possibility when something DID happen that could be. Now am I saying that it was undoubtedly paranormal? No. I am saying that it is, to me, a clear indication of the power and presence of bias on this subject matter. You cannot say THIS never happened but when a qualifying possibility unfolds, decline to look at it as such. And it gets worse...

Tony Rathman posted, on social media within a private group, a short video of a Staticom sitting with annotated words. From my perspective, not only was it a very fruitful session, it was also accurately annotated. An academic personality commented, doubtfully and skeptically, calling into question the methodology itself. Weeks later, same private group, I myself posted my first (and since, last) Staticom video with annotated words. If I am honest, it was not the best clip I've ever shared or attained, but it was good and undeniably had talking being emitted from the data-free white noise. Same academic individual commented on my video, very similarly as to how they did on Tony's – but ended the comment with what may be the world's most long-winded post response, with links, explanations...hell, maybe even a coupon code...this person rambled. But in addition to all of that, they also noted that I should be honest about my limitations of knowledge. Fair enough...this person is not nearly well-versed in my background, studies in areas of sound, physics, etc., which I have been working at diligently for years now...but fine...to them, I am another black-tee-shirt-wearing, ghost-hunting wannabe researcher posting some misleading and misconstrued, sad example of evidence (there, this level of self-degradation should make them happy if they ever read this book). Now what I love about their post commentary is that if you look at the extreme candor as well as poorly disguised honesty, it gets borderline humorous. I'll explain...

This person actually commented twice on mine, unlike Tony's where they rendered a judgment for all to see and know and moved on. The first comment is from where the roots of absurdity, hypocrisy and adaptability can be found. The initial question about the method in use with the word-annotated video was (paraphrasing, which all of this interaction will be summed up by doing), "So are you using something like an Ovilus, or an application with word banks?" Now – why ask if banks full of various words were in play unless...say it with me...you hear words?! Now hold that thought and carry it forward to the next post comment.

In a direct response to my answering post number one, saying, "No word banks are in use. We're generating live white noise at the moment, filtering right then, and then sending the audio through a Bluetooth speaker," this person replied, "Well, then you are not hearing words, but rather nothing more than warbles and artifacts of sound which are a byproduct of the software filtration. I've dealt with someone else on this previously...etc...."

We knew exactly who that other software filtration person they were referring to is, Keith Clark. He was not only the only one doing this when we began doing it, he was WHY we were doing it. Prior to him and us, no one was using the process for ITC, and it was easy to figure this out. Keith is a legend and was a major plus having been someone on our path of DRV development. I have credited his work and influence in at least two of the previous three books I've written. He is truly a pioneer. So we discussed said person, and it was a mutually discouraging experience that we both shrugged off and moved on because it is SO easy to see that this person is operating from a solid foundation of bias. Period. Like, you can see their bias from Google Earth, it's so overblown.

Everyone has a level of bias in all things we assess and consider. We do. Those of us who take paranormality seriously, seriously enough to spend a lot of time on it, get wrongfully and unfairly labeled a "want to or need to believe" types. Those of us who are serious do try not to lean too heavily pro or con, and we have an awareness of where our hearts are on things so we can redirect the navigation to the critical thinking cognitive processing area instead of the emotional sector.

10. Fantastical Feats of the Layperson

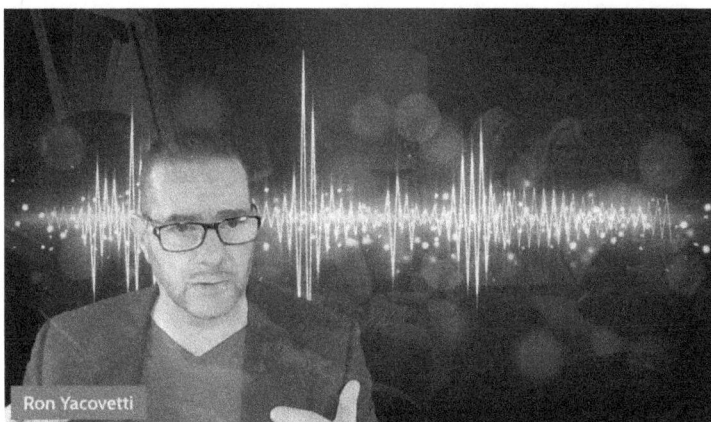

Ron Yacovetti

THIS IS WHERE, if you've not yet figured me out, and I am somewhat of a simple soul, that I march to a unique beat in the ITC world. And whilst I do take pride in educating myself in technology, gadgetry and the like, my unique platform as an ITC operator and researcher is rooted in philosophy. No, I am not a PhD in the field of study. I have studied it in college. I have a BS in communications, and I am a vetted professional in a very unique type of philosophical thought...

satire. It brings with it a radar for hypocrisy, failure to apply continuity of thought, and contradiction. MANY who sling criticisms and snap judgments towards the ITC field do so with holes in their arguments, offenses and, most absurdly, their reasoning. They poop on the idea of continuing consciousness yet study almost no portion of it, if any. They have done little to no in-depth ITC work, and their platform is purely a belief system held in place by bias and its synchronous state with regard to other beliefs and doubts that they hold. In a word...lazy.

So...hard to believe anyone but the elite-level PhD is doing something as fantastical as figuring out how to successfully commune with the deceased, right? This may sound like an abrupt dig, and if it does hit home that way, my apologies. I cannot predict, for all those who will eventually read this book, how they identify, oftentimes, unknowingly and instinctively, but that is how we receive some information, be it music, news or other forms of info.

And it's a strawman argument couched in a criticism and slathered in empty gesture to knock, devalue or dismiss any paranormal research, experimentation or theory on the grounds that they do not possess a PhD or master's from a highly decorated and pricy university when your school of thought...your side of the fence, opposite the layperson, never gave that elusive respect and credit to the pioneers of this research, despite the fact that they ARE/WERE doctors of various sciences or possessed master's degrees or vocational backgrounds so deep that they need a lifeguard. Very Schrodinger's cat of them. When the situation is at a point it must be observed, the outcome and status is decided based on what will keep the layperson unsuccessful and keeping the goal as elusive as possible.

The researcher is subpar, more likely fallible and unreliable unless they have a doctorate or master's, but then when they have it, the phenomena is not legitimate and is not real. Suddenly they hear only warbles and artifacts of sound. It is beyond me why this has been ongoing for so long, but as a genuine philosophical- and satirical-minded person for most of my life, it is beyond white-elephant level of awareness for me. This is why I most often hold a nonchalant attitude towards the academic criteria they say we lack, because there is no winning. In all honesty, it is a mirror image of the same game plan a six-year-old would employ playing a game like tag: whoever reaches ten tags of the other person wins. But then, when YOU get nine tags in the bank, the child then changes the total to twenty tags to win and starts scoring double points on their tags of you. Then there is that tag that didn't count because your foot was on a crack in the driveway, etc. The bullseye, and in our case the prerequisite to be credible, is an incessantly moving target. We are sure not to find and hit it. And if in some instances we do, they disregard it with some improvised excuse for it or disregard it as if it never took place. And these are the folks whose approval I am supposed to seek and need? Did such a level of education, credible mentoring and expertise help the likes of Konstantin Raudive (student of esteemed Carl Jung), Dr. Ernst Senkowski, Dr. Anabela Cardoso? In the minds of those people...not at all. No. So save us all the rhetoric, and unless there is a gateway to unity and progress, those of us genuine laypeople are not interested in being your academic, scientific dancing monkeys for no gain whatsoever.

I am not against, offended by, or opposed in any way to the credibility issue being something taken into consideration. What I am irked by is how it gets more or less important based on aspects of a situation that are not intrinsic to one's ability to assess or understand a specific phenomenon.

As an example, let's say your street holds a block party – a person you've never met before (assume for the example you are newer to the neighborhood) then tells you about a fire in your home. You wouldn't question the skills in the study of fire dynamics, or question if they'd ever been accused of arson, etc. in order to trust the person enough to follow up on the alarming news and take it seriously. So if what makes you think anyone should respond and entertain this claim is the thought, "Well, who wouldn't? That could be the difference between life and death for your loved one"...then it is not the qualifications of the deliverer of the news, it's what you perceive as a loss-potential scenario, and it is THE NEWS or information to be conveyed itself, NOT the same as qualifying the deliverer. Is this information possibly AT ALL important, we decide upon. You can dismiss someone telling you that their Aunt Gertrude is talking to them through a ghost box because there is no risk you perceive to be a valid concern, and that info is honestly of no consequence to you, so IF this not-very-common-to-hear declaration turns out to be false or a miscalculation, you don't really care. The point being that the gravity of the situation, as well as our personal position and bias, determines whether or not we look at the qualifications of who is telling us what they're telling us and how. If our bias is opposed to what they spew verbally, then they'd better be steeped in degrees, scholarships and accolades so when we disagree with them, we at least feel they jumped through enough hoops to deserve to be heard. If we're in sync with their belief system, then, well, "let's hear them out"...community college, Yale, what's the big difference?...they have years of studying the subject (whatever that subject may be). This is all of us...humans, people. It happens. But like any addiction scenario, if you are not aware, you do not acknowledge, then you do not grow, enlighten or serve as a conduit of genuine, honest truths. When the paradigm isn't driving the vehicle with truth-value assessments based on its position versus any hint of objectivity of data, THEN by George, we've got something worth entertaining further.

11. Down Goes Tyson!
A Lovable, Brilliant Man of Science Misinforms the Masses

Image of me in a music video with Dilated Peoples / The Real Rakkaa

So WHILE THIS chapter deals with a less than acceptable social media moment brought to us by the beloved man of science Neil deGrasse Tyson, let's get the obviously odd yet meaningful title of the chapter out of the way and address it first. The phrase was made famous at the end of the fear-provoking era in boxing, where Mike Tyson reigned as the proverbial baddest man on the planet. As is the case with the elite in any competitive sport or activity, their undefeated, unmatched dominance does come to an end. Inevitably, someone younger, newer, smarter, stronger (you get the point) comes along, and your time is up. That's ok. Some never aspire and achieve such, so that in and of itself is amazing. I remember watching when Mike Tyson had that moment thrust upon him against a very underestimated and emotionally charged Buster Douglas. The fight, for those who may not know more than the name Mike Tyson, took place in Japan. The loss, the first of its kind for Mike and arguably one of the biggest upsets in sports history, came by way of brutal knockout. Watching Mike rocked, unable to recover, then fall like a tree was to be forced to absorb the previously unimaginable. It was as momentous as David versus Goliath despite the fact that these were two big heavyweight boxers, and in that division, knowing inevitably one will get hit, you HAVE TO be able to take a shot. Well, until this point, no one had tagged Mike Tyson on the chin clean and hard enough, not to mention unexpectedly enough (it's an old adage in boxing that the shots that hurt the most are the ones you don't see coming) to put him down and especially for the ten count. This remains, arguably, one of the great upsets in sports history. Ok, we now depart from discussing the sweet science (as boxing is known) and return to the applied worldview science.

So, there I was one day, perusing social media, and I take the (for me) very rare glance at TikTok and scroll through a lot of the hoopla and scroll slower when I see stuff that piques my interest in the subject of supernatural types of things. I see a post of what I would easily deem two very brilliant men in a discussion...Joe Rogan and one of the world's favorite science-based personalities, Neil deGrasse Tyson. I enabled the volume on my smartphone, which is often silenced, because while I believe we should all have a voice in this world, I would prefer not to hear some of them. Anyway, the dialog is a pointed and subject-specific one...NDEs, near-death experiences.

Now while I still believe Mr. deGrasse Tyson is likely one of the most brilliant and probably kind people on this planet, his misuse or mistaken use of today's social media platform was really disturbing to me. Incidentally, I label this as misuse or mistaken because what you will see as you read on is that what Neil denies having happened before DID HAPPEN. It IS documented and has been attempted again. It was done under the controls and setting that our worldview bias-happy contingency would want it to be done under, performed by an accredited and brilliant scientist...ya know the stuff they use to discredit anyone without those credentials but ignore the findings of when one DOES possess them.

So I wanted right then and there to include this subject in my next book because I've rambled through three previously written books, about scientism, materialism and the like being cultish and obfuscating results, evidence and data that deserves to be included in theoretical formulation if one is to be balanced in theorizing.

So...the following excerpt from social media is demonstrative of one of two things.

1. Neil deGrasse Tyson spoke on a highly controversial subject without having done tertiary-level web research that could have shown him something he claimed has yet to happen HAD in fact already happened. Or...

2. He knows it took place and instead of addressing it, acknowledging it, and then expressing that he holds a different opinion, outlook or assessment, he flat out acted like it never happened and took advantage of those cult-like followers who just accept the word of the oracle who goes by the title "scientist."

If anything else could have been the explanation for this social media blunder, I am open to hear it. I'd love to be wrong. Here is how it played out, in short...

Neil and Joe are mid-discussion, as social media snippets often go, and Mr. Tyson mentions NDEs, near-death experiences, (sorry to repeat this, but here is where we dive into it) and conflates or fuses the NDE and EOL (end of life) experience by starting out saying "when people have these experiences..." and groups them together as one. Now, while this is not my area of focus in paranormal study, I do try to attain a respectable level of knowledge in connected areas such as psychical phenomena and consciousness, so this already had me on high alert for scientism. An NDE is when someone is clinically dead, even for seconds, then revived and back to living as we know it. An EOL experience is what people report right before they die their physical death, from which they DO NOT return. No one having an EOL experience is telling that tale. It is typically one reported by loved ones or caregivers at the place within which they pass on. See why making them seem synonymous irked me? I know that is wrong, despite any belief in these types of experiences, because it is wrong in a defining, vocabulary and jargon sense...even if one thinks it's all bullshit. I may not believe in Santa Claus anymore, but I do not, nor did I ever, refer to that character as Samuel Clause...because it is not the correct name. Now, I am assuming based on the fact that we are discussing an incredibly brilliant man (Neil deGrasse Tyson), that he knows better and is being dismissive of this stuff by paying little attention to naming convention. I bet he would hate a lecture on splitting "Adams."

At this juncture we're off to a bad start on this, and Mr. Tyson continues...and as he does, I find respect points earned back some because he then does acknowledge it as a purported thing...he called it a thing that happens (a way to avoid any jargon that might connotatively assign credibility to it). He also does quickly breeze by a mention of this has been done...so quickly that I thought he had failed to recognize that until watching it again. So then he goes on to say, "Let's investigate it," pointing out just prior to that statement, how people say they leave their bodies and look back (or down) on themselves. So his declaration to investigate this stuff I was pleased to hear, but then...Neil goes on to state, "That the test for this, to know if one really left their body or was halluci-nating it, is to get some writing on a paper that faces the ceil-ing, and if you truly have floated above your body, you should be able to report back what is written on that paper...and that has yet to happen." Joe Rogan then says inquisitively, "If you get above it." Mr. deGrasse Tyson responds in turn, wrapping up the video, saying, "Yeah...correct. If you get above it...and that has yet to happen."

Here is the point at which I found myself at odds internally, emotionally, because I feel like Neil deGrasse Tyson is not only one of the greatest minds of our time, but also one of those who have the special ability to bridge that academic-layperson partition (to quote the brilliant Mr. Tom Butler). So, this is that moment of truth set up in the opening of this chapter...the big question once again being, "Does he know that it happened, but because this does not gel with his beliefs, biases and opinions, he chose to ignore it under the assumption that most people watching on social media will trust his saying it never happened or not know to question it? OR...does he actually not know yet spoke to something without the minimum of efforts necessary to come across the fact that floating above one's body and reporting back what is on the paper HAS happened?!"

At this point, you may be saying to yourself or me, talking to books is not unprecedented, "Well, you keep saying this has happened. Where is the source or detail to support this?"

Enter Dr. Charles Tart...

Born in 1937, Dr. Charles T. Tart is an American psychologist and parapsychologist known for his psychological work on the nature of consciousness. Right there you now know why it is I, a man with origins as a "ghost hunter," found himself familiar with Dr. Tart. Consciousness and the possible nature of it is our business to learn and know as best we can.

Dr. Tart, working out of the Institute for Transpersonal Psychology in Palo Alto, California, for many years did several experiments on NDEs and OBEs (out-of-body experiences). The one in question and contextually critical now was performed in the 1960s. The subject of the experiment was a young woman whom Dr. Tart anonymously referred to as "Miss Z." She had been a babysitter for his family and had shared unusual sleep experiences that were pretty routine and involved her floating above her body and looking down at it. The experiences, she reported, lasted seconds, but nevertheless, were puzzling to her and very unlike typical dreams she had also experienced from time to time. Important to note, especially for those whose negativity and debunk-happy senses have started seeking to dismiss this, that this young lady had never read anything about OBEs, as this was long before Raymond Moody's book entitled *Life After Life*, which was not available prior to the year 1975, so in essence, she genuinely had no idea what to make of this at all.

Dr. Tart was able to have her spend four nights in his sleep research laboratory, where each night he recorded her electroencephalogram (EEG) in a typical fashion used in dream research that allowed the possibility to distinguish waking, drowsiness, and the various stages of sleep. It was done as strictly as possible, with two channels, frontal-to-vertex and vertex-to-occipital on the right side of the head, recording continuously through the night on a Grass Model VII Polygraph at a speed of ten millimeters per second. Eye movements were measured with a flexible strain gauge taped over one eye, while simultaneously measuring the electrical resistance of her skin using electrodes taped to her right palm and forearm. Two of the four nights' statistics gathered also tracked heart rate and relative blood pressure with an optical plethysmograph (an instrument for recording and measuring variation in the volume of a part of the body, especially as caused by changes in blood pressure) on her finger.

On the first three laboratory nights, Miss Z reported that in spite of occasionally being "out of body," she had not been able to control her experiences enough to be in position to see the target number. Another very important thing to note here is that in making this experiment as vetted as possible, the number written and placed above was different each night. On night four, at precisely 5:57 a.m., there was a seven-minute period of somewhat ambiguous EEG activity.

Then Miss Z awakened, and the moment I sit here bewildered about, that Mr. Neil deGrasse Tyson either ignored, dismissed or outright did not take a moment to learn, as well as denied on social media, actually happened! Miss Z called out over the intercom the target number, which that specific night was the number 25132. It was noted on the EEG recording paper to document the occurrence (Tart, 1968). Dr. Charles Tart also included in his report that the odds against guessing a five-digit number by chance alone are 100,000 to 1, so this was beyond astonishing, as events go, to have taken place.

It was later disclosed that Miss Z had apparently expected Dr. Tart to have propped the target number up against the wall behind the shelf, but when reporting back what that number actually was, she ALSO correctly reported that it was lying flat. Now this is validation of what the number is and how the paper was placed. But again, Mr. deGrasse Tyson seems to avoid or bury this fact. I truly admire him and not only his knowledge but his ability to reach laypersons as well as anyone of science ever has, so I struggle with the idea that he simply was too lazy to take a moment to know if anyone even CLAIMED this experiment had yielded positive results, even if in disagreement with said claims. But if Neil knew of it, why bury it and disregard it as if it had never happened? Credibility protection is a very viable explanation...You see...

Historically, anytime results that rang out as fantastical in nature, both skeptics (you know the cynics who just hijacked the word skeptic) and an abundance of parapsychologists express concerns that these prodigious results may have been hoaxed or even inadvertently produced via fraudulent means. They also assert that, of course, such may simply be rooted in normal sensory channels. Regardless, at this point, I say either do the same level of research on your social media that you would do in your work, or leave the empty declarations and zombie philosophizing to the general public. I found it noteworthy enough to include in this book, which is heavily saturated with more philosophy than ITC works may usually be, because I am acutely aware of not only how many people know and follow Neil deGrasse Tyson, have profile accounts on TikTok but also watch the Joe Rogan podcast. So to see that much outreach regarding what fuels our ongoing battle against accepted worldview scientism, against bias camouflaged by credentials and the fact it is so easily verifiable as untrue, irked the living daylights out of me. Either call out Dr. Tart is unreliable or fraudulent or something, which I AM NOT saying he is at all, but I am saying that it is one thing to not embrace what he did and claims, but quite another to act as if it never happened. Very "emperor's new clothes" of him. Seems the emperor of worldview science lives to prance about in his birthday suit another day.

12. Am I Qualia-Fied?

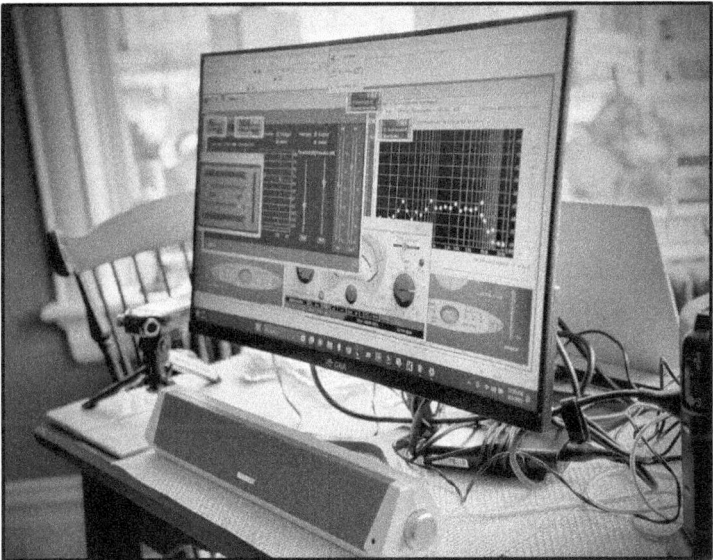

Qualia (singular: quale) is a term that philosophers use to describe the nature, or content, of our subjective experiences. What we are aware of when we see, hear, taste, touch or smell are our qualia. University of Alberta http://www.bcp.psych.ualberta.ca

The concept and existence of qualia are what makes the notion of the brain creating consciousness incredibly difficult to accept and fathom as a rule of scientific law. Very...

Here is where it gets and quite frankly IS difficult...

If the brain creates what we know to be consciousness and all experience happens in our heads, how is it we share some experiences with other people, who themselves would have to be experiencing consciousness created inside THEIR head? Why are we so entrenched in the idea that something physical must birth consciousness? My two cents from what I have read and thought through, especially taking into account all of the experience I've been labeling as paranormal, has me believing that there is a world "out there," and that we do not create all experience in our heads. I find it likely that consciousness is all encompassing and that qualia, or phenomenal experiences that are self-egoic, are what are subjective and individualized. We all perceive, for example, the color red the same. Barring someone with color blindness, we don't argue over the color red, with some standing around the desk of a paint department insisting it is blue or green or otherwise. We see red, and we agree red. But...the things we experience from that which are subjective and personal, those things are where our reflectiveness within our own filtered experience is where we find emotional ties to it: our first red car, a convertible, and the memories of driving it. Or someone may remember the color red as the last shirt or blouse they saw a loved one wearing in the casket on the day of that person's funeral. Those differences, the phenomenal subjective emotions, are not inherent in the perception of the color red from any mechanistic standpoint. These are happenings on the ego-conscious level that take center stage and make themselves known. These are not shared from a position of what we call a collective unconscious, or we would all feel them even if they did not originate within or by us.

Once you look at consciousness as a collective that we are all localized offshoots of, you can see where those ideas of filter hypothesis and its tuning of our brain-transceiver and what we tune into being excitations of consciousness that we reflect upon self-egoically and thus, as a result of it, eclipse the rest of consciousness. Bernardo, whom I should refer to as a blackbelt in metaphors, explains a primo example of such when he points out in *Meaning in Absurdity* that the stars in the night sky are always there and part of our reality and experience even during the day hours...but, that what to us is a great excitation, what our filter focuses on through subjectivity and reflection, those things obfuscate those stars from registering with us at all during daylight. This also explains how what we say lurks in our subconscious is not sub at all, but rather, an obfuscated consciousness that is still shaping, influencing and forming our reality, but most often without our awareness of it. This would explain a lot of what we see as coincidence, incredible timing and more. It also gives me a wider perspective on the data and vocal anomalies we experience with our DRV and now Staticom sessions.

ITC Staticom messages experienced identically while heard by multiple people at a sitting, to me, is also very suggestive of the data and perception being conscious on a collective level (formless state); then through filter hypothesis (or otherwise), we all receive that data/message as perceived auditory information with context, emotion and identical cadence of speech, in the language we all understand. We get the commonalities, but once inside our filter and on the radar of awareness, our individuated states, which will vary per person, give us the personal aspects of it.

Not like one of us versed in more than one language, such as Lourdes being fluent in Spanish and English, is hearing it in Spanish or anything else other than English, while the rest of the group gathered at a Staticom sitting all hear English instead; she too hears English, the shared lingual commonality between us communicatively.

Qualia, the basis for the hard problem of consciousness, is what makes the idea of the brain creating consciousness through neural firings so difficult to accept, because those things are not shared experiences born of shared experiences and individual ones. Most times the nature of experiences are the takeaways for us. Songs in movies that strike chords of emotion are not programmed into the song or its characteristics, yet some tunes will trigger shared identical excitations within our awareness while others will hit individuals in ways very personal and specific to them. The oldish movie *Vision Quest*, starring a young Matthew Modine, profiled a coming-of-age and also Rocky-like feel centered around a high school wrestler. Now, for the romantic types, the love story may be the big takeaway. But for the wrestlers in many of us, those who took to the mat at an early age, that whole making of a champion, overcoming the daunting task that has eluded all others who dared try it, THAT is, for us, the take-away. Same movie, same soundtrack but our self-egoic, reflective experience from it, that which reverberates and echoes within us, THAT is our qualia in action.

13. Brother, Can You Spare a (Para)Dime?

Paradigm (Para-Dime): In science and philosophy, a paradigm is a distinct set of concepts or thought patterns, including theories, research methods, postulates, and standards for what constitute legitimate contributions to a field. The word paradigm is Greek in origin, meaning "pattern," and is used to illustrate similar occurrences.

– Wikipedia

ONE OF THE big issues for those within the paranormal field speaking out into the world, their tales, experiences and more, is that the worldview most abide by, knowingly or not, is not a place within which such information is deemed welcomed or, especially, credible. But why? Most folks who scoff at anything paranormal have NOT experimented, experienced or even tried to participate in it, yet they adamantly do not believe in the possibility of ANY of it. Did we learn nothing from our mom asking us, "'How do you know that you don't like vegetables if you never even try them?" This has always amazed me, well, most particularly since I began investigating the paranormal. It was just an unfounded, gut feeling that it cannot be true, does not make sense, and hence they laugh at it, joke about it, and dismiss it. Arrogance in the living is also quite underrated, wouldn't you agree?

So, at this point, you have also probably heard or read my rantings about the presence of bias and its off-the-rails causation when it is what fuels the thinker...any thinker. We all have them, and we all must work to allow for them while not letting them drive, from the backseat or front.

I have also come to realize, as have my Staticom partners, that if we are to make a serious impact to ITC and its research, to do the whole "shift or changing of a paradigm," we must first not only know what a paradigm is, but also precisely as much as possible about the one we seek to change. This has always been something that has historically seen morphing and remodeling over great lengths of time. Never, to my knowledge (and I realize I do not have all of the answers here) has it been a revolutionary thing that just happens with explosive spontaneity. So in essence what I am describing is a movement. We have seen those play out in civil rights, gender rights and more, where leaders influence and collect those who are like-minded. They work as one, in lockstep, gradually trying to bring their cause to light. As younger generations get on board, you can begin to see the changes most commonly held by most people you come into contact with... but not all.

The idea of being like-minded, or in instances where the congregating of many is rooted in a goal or purpose, may also be referred to as "hive minded." Like bees or even more so like ants that run in colonies (but better not run in my house or it's Raid time!), there is a lack of impactful power associated with the individual, but the collective is a much different and very transformative entity as a whole. Not to present too broad a stroke in painting the picture here, and to remain as close contextually to the spooky stuff as possible, let us look at what the collective sides on a massive scale would be. In the most elementary and basic way, ghosts, spirits and paranormal phenomena exist in reality, or they absolutely do not. In arguing between these sides, especially in the field, the proverbial sea of black tee-shirts, I can't help but wonder if anyone ever realizes how they ended up on the side they are now on. Do you, the reader, realize what leads you to what you think, feel and deem to be correct when the paranormal stuff is discussed or debated? Should we not all have a coherent idea that we can iterate when it comes to this?

Not to get too deep philosophically, but you know I probably will now, anyway...The first thing to realize is that in the cut-and-dry laying out of two sides, the believers and the nonbelievers, is the inherent principle of bivalence. The concept of what any declaration about the field seems to hold with regard to truth-value, given one's worldview, means everything as to where we end up, on which side of that divide.

In any one of our opportunities to explain ourselves, our position and why we hold it, almost all of us, if not all of us, would explain that our accepted paradigm is based on logic and truth as we perceive it. But in actuality, as many great philosophers such as Thomas Kuhn would attest, some of those pieces are not in that precise order at all.

Our adopted paradigm, Dr. Kastrup will suggest, in agreement with Mr. Kuhn, plays a very unique and to most, underlying role. The paradigm itself, they explain, does not allow for the aggregation and interpretation of "objective data" outside of said paradigm at all. The data in question cannot be neutral. In fact, they go on to say, it is the paradigm that steers science folk towards or away from things in the world that are capable of being measured, and cherry-picking which of the countless things under this umbrella hold any relevance whatsoever and, if so, how much. The paradigm is not forged from the parts, as a reductionist mind might believe, but instead it serves as a filter and sensory overlay to categorize, classify and dismiss data based on what is synchronous with it. Imagine a house choosing which bricks can and cannot be included to hold it up. That's absurd! Dr. Kastrup notes that the brilliant William James stated that, *"The paradigm itself determines which explanations for observed facts are acceptable or to be preferred."* See why it is pretty much an insurmountable task to try to overturn or influence a paradigm within individuals purely by sharing our paranormal evidence?

The great science philosopher Thomas Kuhn noted in one of the best books I've read, *Meaning in Absurdity* by Dr. Bernardo Kastrup, that, "Paradigms change over time (something we all may think 'well of course' about), and along with them, that which science considers to be true or reasonable." Of that statement, one might think, "Well, that sounds right. It's called progress. We move forward. We learn and advance and form new ideas built on the lessons we've learned." Ok, so here is the next unexpected point of derailment for us.

The word progress, which would be a choice we would all make in that previous statement, means to move forward in a linear fashion with a sense of what Dr. Kastrup refers to as a "continuous refinement." We have a modality, we learn, study, experiment and evolve it to a new and better version of it. Well, no...not quite how it goes.

Historically, science has not executed on the notion of continuous refinement, but rather skipped around the logistical wheel of chance and shifted position based on a variety of things. Oftentimes the result is a paradigm and set of beliefs that were once the mockery-laden ideas of the modern-day quack, suddenly now profound, deep and exalted in their status amongst the educated and elite. I believe today in politics they call that flip-flopping, or hypocrisy or...go ahead and say it...bullsh*t, flat out.

Now, those who may be feeling a little iffy about that, after all, this is SCIENCE we're talking about here, may be asking, "Can you even name or point out one good example of this happening throughout history?" Indeed, I can.

Sir Isaac Newton, when first postulating that gravity was/is "...an intrinsic force, innately acting between bodies at great distance, and irreducible to contact between cells," he was a laughingstock within the realm of accepted science. His work and ideas were branded as occultish, magical in nature and flat-out nonsensical metaphysics, yet years later Newton and his whimsical theory of crazy talk would be placed in science's version of a "hall of fame" – and perhaps much like I mentioned Mr. deGrasse Tyson disregarding the viable data collected on NDE by Dr. Charles Tart, this act of shaming would be wiped away like water-soluble ink on a dry-erase board.

And make no mistake here, I do not relish writing about this or find it to be the "Gotcha!" moments I wrote previously that, my son's mom used to point out, motivated me in debates. I do this for the same reason I pose challenges to judgments about our hearing mechanisms, visual mechanisms and sensory input when we accumulate and interpret paranormal data, or what we believe to be...to spark thought. If you read everything I have written in every book I've done and find you agree with little to none of my ideas and concepts, that is not a failure to me. I am not trying to influence or sway, but rather share what I've learned...hence my mentions of people like Dr. Kastrup or Ruper Sheldrake or Thoman Kuhn. These people deserve not only the respect of being mentioned but the opportunity to become familiar to others when they engage in thought, debate and presentations about the unknown.

Honestly, I don't even know for certain if any or all of them would be one hundred percent, or any number shy of that, behind my views and assessment of paranormal data. But they have done to and for me what it is I hope to do to and for you, which is push the bounds of what you know, think you know, and more importantly...WANT to know.

So, it is good to perhaps remember when throwing out what seems or, to you, is logical in arguing about the paranormal that our position or paradigm rules how we see what we see and accept, to birth that logic we wield like a weapon and a calling card.

It is very funny to me that in the beginning of my ITC endeavors as an enthusiast, I was purely an operator. I bought a device someone else who was clearly talented and brilliant made; I learned how to use it (and how not to) and then enjoyed my sessions wherever I could hold them. I wondered if I should learn, venture out into the realm of the ghost box builder. It didn't feel like me. Suddenly, I have the patience and firsthand ability to intuit what to do and why? I don't think so. This is not to say that I avoided educating myself on how all of those things work. I did. This was like landing the coaching role by design and not taking to the field amongst a sea of colorful helmets. You still need to know the game and the rules, so I made sure I did.

What was in a way an inadequacy as an ITC guy, not being a builder, led me to find my path in DRV and, eventually, Staticom. For that, I am grateful and look at that lesson in building on our strengths and not wallowing in our shortcomings. Why do I bring this up now, you may wonder. Me too. What do I even mean? Ok, I kid. I know why...here goes... Because it led me to construct a philosophy. Not having a philosophy with these things, to me, is to have a ton of stuff and absolutely nowhere to put it; so it just gets strewn out across your whole life path. Cumbersome, I assure you.

This is an aspect of what we do that I think, much like studying consciousness, is understudied and less than adequately learned. I'll turn to examples inspired by one of our most gifted minds in philosophy to illustrate this in a structural way: Dr. Bernardo Kastrup.

You see, when people who scoff at the paranormal do so, they are coming from a place where what they feel they know to be sensible and true, unlike magical and fantastical ideas may seem, leads them to conclude what you are saying is not logical. That is a routine often played out in our internal and external communications about what we do. Dr. Kastrup points out that much of our logic is rooted in what is referred to as "the principle of bivalence": an idea that suggests that any idea about the world or any aspect within it has a determinate truth-value. In this notion, the foundation is that anything stated must either be true or false despite whether or not we can ever know for sure which one it is. How's that for requiring an open mind? Couched in this concept is the idea that, due to bivalence, if two ideas seem to be opposed and not in harmony, then one MUST be true and the other false. But it is these contemporary philosophies as well as those before them that make clear the possibility that both can be true or false. Hopefully, as I delve into this perhaps unanticipated road in a book about ITC and spirit contact, you are starting to see its importance. Unless one truly does not care to know the most they can or what those who with little to know experience or experimentation have to say about this paranormal stuff, it should now be clear why this thought-mapping process of having and knowing one's philosophy is vital.

Now, hold on a minute, logic Ron, you are saying it is bad to have or use or apply? No, no, no...I am not. I am saying we need to understand what fuels it, constructs it and sustains it. At this point, we now know that our accepted paradigm hovers over it like an overcast sky, affecting how everything beneath it is and can be viewed. And we know that bivalence is a governing factor in how we decide what is true, oftentimes choosing based on paradigm-acceptable data. But logic itself, as we understand it, is critical to convey our thoughts, reasoning and more. Ideally, we find a way to wield it without the infusion of bivalence. But to do that, we need to know what brings bivalence to the dance, even if on an awareness level none of us would welcome it. And that, folks like Mr. Kastrup point out, can be done by employing different axioms.

Axioms, to brush up on it, being statements or propositions that are regarded as being established, accepted, or self-evidently true, require no justification by us; they just are... period. So would we have a better grip on this whole reality thing if we cease the inclusion of axioms that allow bivalence and replace them with open-minded and fair concepts that, as an institutionalist would feel, do not prove out or disprove anything by proving or disproving something else. Truth and falsity do not establish each other; each can coexist or need to be broken out to display in and of themselves.

Ron Yacovetti

Something you all might find intriguing, as did I, was how bivalence not only may seem like it is unavoidable, but also is a fully valid axiom. Surely, as we have been raised to think, something is either true or not. Paradox is where this all takes an odd turn, and I am only taking a little time to showcase this because framework, thought process and how we map it out to others is the only way we redirect and rework the debate about the legitimacy of paranormality.

Take, for example, what Bernardo's book *Meaning in Absurdity* references as the Liar Paradox. In that masterful book, he gives an abbreviated version of it: "**This statement is not true.**" This is where it gets fun and confusing. If this statement is in fact true, then what it says of itself is true, and that means it must be false. One of the major lessons in making you aware of this, as I myself have now become, is to illustrate that our linear, continuous, self-referencing, bivalent ways are not the only way to see things and really show us how being open-minded can look. This avenue into the philosophy of life, the bizarre and more does force us to not just accept the way most of those who attack the paranormal and those who do not know how to properly defend it may think. It gets deep. What about this statement where bivalence is not a welcome aspect? "**The following statement is true. The preceding statement is not true.**" See what I am saying here? This, also compliments of Mr. Kastrup, shows that we cannot approach that age-old cliche "Are ghosts real?" or "Do you believe in ghosts?" question the same way anymore, or we get nowhere. The cynic and the proponent of paranormality both find themselves at a stalemate with this, which may explain in some ways why the

118

cynic loads the debate with circular reasoning and presupposed ideas that materialist science and its physics state with absolution. Perhaps. The realization that it is not all cut and dry, one way or the other or...say it with me...true OR false only...that realization is our gateway to the next era of thinkers in paranormality's ongoing growth to potentially being normality.

14. ITC's Prominent Methodologies
A Very Brief Side-by-Side Analysis

HERE ARE a few technical and functional differences in how these two means of communicating with spirits size up to each other. Having spent years using both means, a sweeping ghost box (the modern standard to most in the paranormal field) and DRV, direct radio voice, I have come to realize key differences in both viable methods.

Ghost Box Operation: Most often one-to-three-word answers (if you average it out). A brevity to the messages we (the Staticom Project Team) feel is due to the methodology itself and its sweeping a radio band whilst white noise itself is likely the conduit. In any case...when a partial word is heard...

Academia studies will show that the brain completes or fills in the remaining part or syllables of the given word. This may be true in some instances...It's an aspect of how they discredit or dismiss sweeping radios as NOT being legit ITC. The ghost box user is essentially forced to acknowledge that possibility and has no rebuttal because the other argument used against them is that there are words fragmented like audio artifacts from which the completion of partial words stem. Human vocals or the identical type of speech is the anomaly sought after, so the other side of the belief barrier suggests that you are essentially peeing in the pool within which you swim with this method because you are infusing human vocals, and thus, most operators and enthusiasts worldwide cannot discern between a voice from beyond and, well...a voice. It is this and only this aspect of ghost box use that irks and concerned me from early on in my paranormal days. Why? Because I knew I believed in its being able to work. I witnessed it firsthand and did not like to allow discrediting statements to go unattended. I too was force-fed this hard-to-digest fact, just the same.

The DRV Operator is also forced to acknowledge that such can happen where their mind completes a partial word in order to make sense of what's being heard. This remains a small possibility within which instances where artifacts may be forged during the method and be mistaken for fragments of words. However, at a closer look, one could discern that the depth of sound usually identifying vowels, consonants and diphthongs in human speech are not present in artifact-born audible sounds. They can be distinguished from speech. But what IS unique to the DRV (and now Staticom) operator is the fact that they can still use context should it be part of a small phrase or a large sentence or more. The methodology, not limited to the same brevity of message that a sweeping box may be, does produce context in the form of thoughts and ideas conveyed, as opposed to one- or two-word responses. So the DRV/Staticom approach, which is predicated on the rock-solid foundation that it is not sweeping radio broadcasts, brings with it a huge bonus to its authenticity: that there are no human vocals involved at all. Especially with the white-noise generator replacing the mediumistic role that the radio once held, we are forced to realize that the undeniable anomaly is that THERE ARE VOICES SPEAKING... PERIOD. None should be present at all.

15. We Win AND Lose by Knockout!?

Do Spirits Return?

USING A RADIO TO COMMUNICATE

GONYAC PARANORMAL

PRESENTS

THE DIGITAL SÉANCE INITIATIVE

Yes – read that title again, and again, and again if you need to, in an attempt to understand it. Does it seem to make sense? No. If I were the reader and not the writer of it, knowing where this is going, I too would not think this is a sensible statement. But does it even seem to contextually make sense? To be honest, I would concede...not yet. But just wait...you have no idea how appropriate that is to the land-scape we paranormalists face every day.

So here's the thing...In our never-ending efforts, endeavors and defensive situations, we the believers in things outside of the accepted cult-minded science have to or are asked to provide proof of what we think and believe. Proof, another loaded and supremely subjective thing to discuss, will vary per person asking for it, like the amount of food sufficient to feel like one's money's worth will vary per individual at an all-you-can-eat buffet. What is enough for some, not even close for others. And like the role of the consumer AT the buffet, those asking for this proof are never fully satisfied or satiated in their appetite for comfort in the discussion. So it is safe to assume there is never enough proof of this ghostly stuff...right? Guys? Anyone still there? HA! You get the message. There SHOULD be and could be a level of adequate proof, but those who are most often at the helm of the "SS *Prove it to me*" are also virtually NEVER open to the idea of paranormality at all. So they want you to step up, share and explain your data, trends and more, only to still think it all bullshit because you CANNOT, to their moving target of standards, EVER hit a bullseye and change their logic, which is affixed by their paradigm.

These people seek to disarm, discredit and dismiss those who are willing to take the bait and argue their cause. I myself am not unwilling, but I would not approach this from the posi-tion of the defense in a trial. I would start by removing the foundation of bivalence in all applied ideas of logic and reason, in seeking truths, in order to make my points. This is, of course, another discussion and possibly book altogether, but mentioned because I think we need to look at putting dents in the paradigms of those people from the framing of the discussion, not by entering it under their terms and accepted ideas like a visiting team playing on someone else's home field. This is a big deal, and like the sports world's big deals, say the Super Bowl, it is played in a neutral space. So in the debate about the legitimacy of paranormality, that neutral place must be found and agreed upon as a fair space by the cynic and investigator...not just one or the other.

Now...here's where the backbone for this odd-titled chapter comes in. When these folks request everything we have to show this is an EVP from spirit or a manifestation of a ghost, etc., they do not expect us to be able to change their tune. That's time waste number one. BUT...what happens when we put forth data or files or clips that are irreproachable or inexplicable to anyone with any position on paranormal stuff? When it cannot be clearly explained away. Remember, to debunk is not to suggest another possibility but to show that it WAS something else. So what I find crazy in all of this and why I will pick my moments and battles and stances to make is this...

We truly WIN or LOSE by knockout.

This phrase I once again borrow from my years in the fight industry because it was the first thing that came to mind when I realized the landscape upon which all of this para stuff plays out. If you have ever watched a prizefight...boxing or MMA (mixed martial arts) and in what was supposed to be a well-matched bout between two combatants, it instead turns out to be a one-sided destruction of one of them, there are immediate judgments cast about it. Harsh ones. Speculative and harsh comments abound across the web-scape of sports pages covering that event. But why?

Simple...it was not even or played out with any ebb and flow to it. It was visibly what seemed like a HUGE mismatch... and yes, I am getting to the point.

In terms of the paranormalist and evidence presentation to others, both believers and cynics alike, it is that same suspicion triggering modality. When something performs or seems so, so very good and compelling, people doubt it, even those who call themselves "ghost hunters." Some could be jealous, yes. But others, once it reaches a level surpassing the standard or commonly attained levels of quality and provability, people jump to doubting it is even real. "Surely they're hoaxing it" or "That's totally faked and being done by...(fill in the blank)."

Now, I think you know what I am saying by this unfair and ridiculous scenario we find ourselves in and why I personally will not take the bait to work on proving myself to most people. I know I am doing honest work, not hoaxing and certainly not trying to profit from fraud. My sense of genuine self-integrity gives me comfort, and I move on unscathed by these folks.

So we either fall short of sufficiently compelling, vetted and credible data on a given subject, case or file...OR...we bring the heat, make the point supremely compelling and arouse suspicion of foul play and falsification. We win or lose by knockout. It is almost inescapable UNLESS the people we interact with are genuinely looking for truth, understanding and are willing to let their gut tell them that the person presenting information is or seems credible enough to entertain the truth they profess about it. I hate to use the words open mind, because it also gets tossed around a lot by those who don't even display a shred of it, but preach it since it is cool and trendy to do so.

My advice here? Pack the punch of proof with the best data you can collect and capture. Present it as you can do such and be open to other people's suggestions. If you walk in integrity and with a standard of excellence you hold yourself to in all that you do, then you can more easily identify those who are sharing ideas to help or contribute and those who are incessantly looking for why you cannot be and should not be right about any of it.

16. The Voices of Entity Voices
My Beloved Teammates Share Their Personal Paranormalization Journeys

**Lourdes Gonzalez –
GonYac
Paranormal/DRV/ITC
& Staticom
Researcher**

IT's funny how things come around full circle. How my experiences as a child would help me later in life in what we do today. I come from a family background that studied and still studies Espiritismo. What is Espiritismo, you may ask? It is the Spanish and Portuguese word for Spiritism, which is the belief that good and evil spirits can affect health, love, luck and other aspects of human life. Espiritismo is most popular in the Caribbean and Latin America.

Growing up as a child, most of my family practiced Espiritismo. My mom, being the youngest of ten children, did not practice, but we did attend family ceremonies on a regular basis. At the age of eight, since I was around the practice all my life, I was quite comfortable seeing my aunt and cousins being completely taken over by spirit, allowing full control of their body by the entity. After the ceremony was over, the person taken over by spirit had no memory of the events that had transpired.

One normal Espiritismo ceremony evening, or so I thought, after the protection and blessing ritual for the children (which was my favorite part of the ceremony, by the way), I experienced something that terrified me. My cousin, who was under the influence of spirit, accidentally bumped into my mom, and all of a sudden, the spirit then jumped into my mom. As I stated earlier, my mom did not practice, so seeing my mom under the influence of spirit terrified me. I had never experienced my mom being under the control of spirit. My family immediately took my brother and me into another room and then proceeded to remove the spirit. Fascinatingly, when this ordeal was all over, my mom had absolutely no recollection about what had happened. What is even more intriguing is that to this day, she still does not have any memory of it. After all these years, I still have no idea what was done to remove that spirit from my mom. For many years after that, I shied away from anything paranormal until I met Ron in 2016.

My passion for the paranormal has been increasingly growing since I've met Ron Yacovetti. We have investigated many locations throughout the years, learning new methods and techniques from other investigators, and it has helped me to embrace the paranormal instead of running from it. I feel grateful for that. I feel blessed to have the opportunity to help others with our method of communication, Staticom. When someone's loved one comes through and you see how much it means to the person who is receiving the message, it's the best feeling in the world not only for that individual, but for us as well. And for that, I thank you, Ron Yacovetti. I love you!

Tony and Cherie Rathman – Entity Voices/DRV/ITC & Staticom Researchers

We never expected the world of the strange and unusual to become our everyday norm, but it has. It has become such a common everyday occurrence that we no longer even bat an eye at the newest turn of events that we confront from day to day. It is by no means to say we are not fascinated, intrigued and mind blown still today by what occurs, but that it is more of the under-standing that the largest set of variables involved in creating paranormal activity are outside of our realm of knowledge, that the conditions, the variables, or just plain free will of spirits to act or communicate with us is completely within their control, and since this cannot be forced and has to happen within these gray areas of the unknown, we can do no more than to ask and wait to see what happens.

We never expected our life to be so heavily focused on discovering the afterlife. Maybe Cherie might have had a more profound interest in the beginning, as I was a complete skeptic and nonbeliever of the paranormal until she took (or in my case forced) me on the paranormal journey.

My father was a physics, chemistry, and physical science instructor, and even the simplest of questions as a child were always answered in a scientific fashion. Dad, why is the sky blue? Well, the sky looks blue because the molecules in the air scatter broadband white light, which contains every color in the rainbow, and each color travels on its own special type of wave, called its wavelength. These molecules in the air scatter blue light from the Sun more than they scatter red light due to its short choppy wavelength, making the color we most easily see during the scattering blue.

Paranormal occurrences are not widely accepted by most scientific studies, although great strides have been made in the last ten years to acknowledge many of the principles those of us use in the research community of the paranormal and have been trying to show for decades. Paranormal phenomena cannot be replicated to the point that science needs to study it. It cannot be brought into a lab to be studied and replicated using the scientific method; plus the scientific method is based on our 3D world under which we live and is the evaluation of this world based on the body's sensual perceptions and cognitive evaluations of the results of this 3D world. It would appear to me that what we call today paranormal may be nothing more than the normal, but that which falls far outside our bodily senses, understanding, and physical rules that govern the 3D world in which we live.

Having grown up indirectly with sciences governing most of my outlook on the world around me, I was a bit taken aback when I met my wife, Cherie, and found her fascinated with the paranormal shows that began to hit the airwaves. "Come watch this with me," she would yell from the living room.

"You will love this." But I did not. I found it no more than fabricated entertainment for the point of high television ratings and could not sit through more than a couple of minutes. If these EVPs were so easy to catch, why didn't more people have evidence of this? If spirits could do this much interacting with objects and devices, why was the concept of the afterlife still so unknown? This was only for ratings, and at the time, that was what I truly believed. Until the day my wife, Cherie, tricked me into doing something different for Valentine's Day.

Normally we would head to a resort in Phoenix and relax for the weekend by the pool, drinking, laughing, and swimming. But this year she wanted to do something different. "What would you like to do?" I asked. She stared directly into my eyes and said, "I want to go ghost hunting." I thought, *What a waste of time and money, where the heck are we going to go, and what on earth does she see us doing even if we find a so-called haunted location?* Well, I had two choices considering this was a Valentine's Day request. I could find a way to honor her request, or I could have her upset with me until next Valentine's Day. The choice was clear what I needed to do. I got online, and to my surprise there was a hotel in downtown Phoenix that had a reputation for being haunted. I thought, *Perfect*, and made a reservation for the weekend. There, I did it, I completed her request, or so I thought until I began thinking about what it was she was going to do to capture any paranormal evidence.

The people on the shows had equipment they were using. I did another Google search for what type of equipment paranormal investigators use, and the typical responses came back as being a night-vision digital camera, a digital recorder, and an EMF or electromagnetic frequency reader, so I bought my wife these three components. Now she had a place to investigate for the weekend and equipment to use. I was happy not necessarily to investigate, but because I knew my wife would be happy, as this was what she'd requested and wanted.

So we spent the weekend at the Hotel San Carlos, and I played along all weekend. I investigated with her, asked questions for her, and I could see that she was both having fun and enjoying this new adventure. That was all that mattered to me, that she was enjoying her Valentine's Day, and I was making that happen for her. So the weekend went well, and that was all I was expecting, until we got home and my wife started to review the photos, the recordings, and the video captures. She was calling me over every five minutes. "What is in this photo? That was not there when I took the picture." I could not answer her. "Listen to this; whose voice is this on the recorder? You and I were the only two people in the basement." I could not answer her. I did not know whose voice was on the recorder answering the question that was asked. There was no one else there when we recorded this, and my mind began to spin, searching for reasonable and rational explanations for how this was happening.

By the time my wife had finished the review of all her devices, I had about twenty-five or thirty pieces that I just completely could not explain. Photo, video, and audio recordings with strange objects in them or audio answers that I could not for the life of me understand how they got there. I spent months trying to explain how these got there, and finally said, "I can't explain these. Let's go back and try again to see if there is strange lighting in the photo, or sounds coming from a wall or connecting room that could explain how these ended up on the recording."

We went back and investigated again, new unexplained voices and strange occurrences in the photos and videos appeared, and once again I could not account for why. Even having paid special attention to our surroundings and what could cause issues with lighting or sounds. We went back again and again until our total number of investigations of this hotel reached over fifty times. Each time new and unexplained things were captured, and the voices we received on the audio over those fifty times began to become familiar to us, and names were even given on the recorder as to whom we were talking with.

I was not ever able to give a rational explanation for where the voices came from, only that they continued to answer our questions. I was fascinated with the photos and video captures, but the audio answers stood out to me as the most prevalent, as they showed both comprehensive understanding of the questions we were asking and showed intelligence in the responses that were given. We also found it fascinating that from the voice we could achieve a mountain of information before we even heard the response to our question. We could determine whether it was a man or a woman answering. We could determine if it was an adult or a child; we could hear if they had an accent or territorial dialect in their words; we could tell their emotional state by the way the response was said. We could tell if they were happy or sad, upset, angry or depressed, and all this information could be obtained before we even heard what response was given.

This was the start of paranormal investigation for Tony and Cherie Rathman and has now continued for the last thirteen years. Our focus was placed on audio communication, beginning with EVP and then expanding to ITC spirit box communication, and today has moved to ITC and our newest development with Ron and Lourdes of the Staticom communication method.

Paranormal has become our normal, and the experiences and interactions over the last thirteen years have been nothing but extraordinary and a few times a bit scary, but the fear of the unknown is a stated fact, so we would always tell ourselves, you fear because you don't understand, not because of something else. So we would continue forward, and today has us developing communication that should literally make the paranormal community take a second look at the methods they are currently using.

We would never trade the experiences and information we have learned from investigating paranormal, and although still today we take criticism from nonbelievers and skeptics and sometimes even from academics, we would not change this path and know we will continue to research and investigate the paranormal until the day we pass over to the other side. Know that if Cherie and I are on the other side, we will be looking to communicate with those of you here running methods of spirit communication that we may have had an opportunity to help develop while we were alive.

**Chris Allgood –
Southern Entities /
EVPI / EVP Specialist**

I have been what I call a "sensitive" since as far back as I can remember – my first experience was at five when I was playing with a little boy in a cemetery. I later discovered I was the only one who knew he was there. I have felt, heard, sensed, and responded to this energy my entire life as far back as I can remember.

My most profound experience happened when I was twelve. I came face-to-face with a full-body apparition that appeared to be trying to communicate with me, but I could not hear the woman talking even though I could see her transparent facial expressions and mouth moving as she tried to tell me her story. The experience scared me beyond belief to the point I closed off my senses so I did not have to feel that intense fear again.

My father taught us growing up when something scares or intimidates you, it has beaten you. Being the type of person who will not allow myself to be beaten or intimidated by anyone or anything, I decided to face my fears. I started looking for spirits anywhere I could and going to any place rumored or known to be haunted. Just so I could find out why I could see and sense the things I could.

High school was when I thrived on haunted locations. I would drag my friends anywhere in the middle of the night, during the day, or anytime possible that had spirits or someone said was haunted...I was there. I would point and say, "Do you see that?" I would speak out and say, "Did you guys hear that?" Most of the time they hadn't or wouldn't admit it, but when they did, it caused a flurry of high schoolers running like an ice-cream truck had just passed a park full of kindergartners with change falling out of their pockets. They ran as fast as they could to get away but then stood in amazement once they reached the getaway car. They could not figure out why I stood my ground, asking questions as if someone would respond.

This continued into my twenties, and at twenty-four I bought a recorder and camera and started my journey into para-normal investigating. Like other paranormal investigators, I now have many pieces of equipment. The paranormal consumes my life now outside of my professional life – para-normal is now my normal. When I investigate, I place my equipment where I feel the energy, and I get great results. I stop and chat with the energy as it comes to me. I feel it, hear it, or even see it standing in front of me. I have done private homes and received messages while in the homes. I have been given an address and relayed information to the sender that I could not possibly have known. I have seen spirits look at me, run from me, and even speak to me, somehow knowing that I know they are there. I spend every day knowing what we are all trying to prove by doing investigations. There are energies that walk among us; they are energies that were once human that have left their bodies behind and left our physical realm. They have intelligence, consciousness and sometimes know we are there to communicate with them.

Now let's take a step back, even experiencing all the metaphysical things that I have experienced my entire life – feeling, hearing, seeing, and sensing the things I do in the paranormal – I struggle in my own mind. You see, I am now fifty years old, and in my non-paranormal life by profession I have a very experienced thirty years of construction. I have been in the window and door business my entire thirty-year career. I was also a law enforcement officer for ten years. I have a data-driven, fact-based mindset and training that has been drilled into my conscious thought patterns. You would think metaphysical, data-driven, and fact-based mindsets would compete with each other in the paranormal. Believe me, sometimes they do, because at times I feel insane with what I hear, feel, see, and sense.

You will hear me preach "situational awareness" on *Entity Voices Paranormal Evidence*. Situational awareness is defined in a couple of different ways.

Law enforcement uses situational awareness as this:

> "Situational awareness is knowing where you are and what is going on around you, allowing individuals and organizations to be more alert and informed and to make better decisions. For organizations, this includes awareness about personnel location and assigned duties, the environment, and any potential risks.

> "Understanding the warning signs of danger, the potential for flight or assault, and gauging the seriousness and level of danger in any given situation."

The other definition is as such:

> "The perception of environmental elements within a volume of time and space, the comprehension of their meaning, and the projection of their status in the near future."

Situational awareness to me is a couple of different things. I apply all the above and throw in my background in construction and windows and doors to allow me to access and disprove or prove evidence. For example, when I or someone else captures a picture of a shadow figure, I pay close attention to the details surrounding the figure. The walls, doors and windows also captured in the picture can determine the height. If a doorway captured in the photo is a standard six-foot, eight-inch door and the shadow figure only stands about three-quarters of the way in the door frame, that tells me the figure is approximately between four to five feet tall. My experience has also helped with mist photos. Knowing the construction materials and climate of the area where the photo was taken, it is easy to determine if the materials, weather, time of day or location would cause a natural fog or mist in the photo. When you can rule out all those things, there is nothing left to determine other than you caught a paranormal anomaly.

Having the knowledge I have from being involved in construction and law enforcement has given me the knowledge-based information to determine in a location the hazard and conditions that will cause false evidence upon review or while analyzing others' evidence, because I do not miss any details. Being a sensitive also keeps me from going crazy when I am standing next to a power panel or breaker box in a dark house. I feel the energy coming from the man-made materials but have the understanding to debunk it with my construction background and understand layouts of electricity patterns within the location. I have created a fact-based, data-driven metaphysical mindset in the paranormal world that keeps me sane and tells me when they have crossed that veil to communicate. God has given me abilities to see more than most and the attention to detail to know when the paranormal really exists; that is my "situational awareness"!

The paranormal field we live in today has changed so much in the twenty-five or so years I have been engulfed in it. Back when I began, it was the fear of the unknown and the running caused by the door slam or anomalous voice heard. Today more and more people are driving in full force to investigate. People are more brazen and bolder, and when they hear a voice, they start asking questions to see if they get answers.

Technology is taking the place of review because responses are being heard in real time. Staticom allows and has proven that these entities we are hearing can communicate through space and time no matter where you are. We all know aliens exist, and the government is starting to admit it. Bigfoot has been sighted multiple times, but never has anyone produced concrete evidence. In the paranormal world there are so many investigators who can produce thousands of pictures, video and audio evidence of entities that respond intelligently, act with a purpose, and seem to have a consciousness or free will to interact with the investigators. Then at the same time we have skeptics, disbelievers and scientists who say they don't exist. I believe the paranormal world is on the edge and has the data to back up the existence of life after death, and soon it will be accepted. Of course, there will always be those who go to church and pray to God and say ghosts don't exist...if they do not exist, then please send me God's address so I can get the answer straight from him myself.

**Audra Keeler –
Southern Entities –
EVPI / EVP Specialist**

Boy, do I have a story to tell you! If you come across anyone in the paranormal community, you are bound to hear something along those lines, on how they got started in this field. My story is slightly different. Yes, it started in my childhood like many others; no, I did not see any ghosts. I had nightmares. The kind that make you jolt upright in bed and can still clearly remember some forty-odd years later.

I grew up in Northwest Ohio, was born in the '60s, and spent my childhood in the '70s. Back then, there were not any iPhones, YouTube videos, DVDs, or even VHS tapes to watch a scary movie on. I bring up this point to state that there was not much data for my brain to come up with the horrible dreams that I had. Nothing to feed my creative juices for having such thoughts, that, and there was no way my parents would let me watch anything scary. What fourth grader do you know dreams of saving children and fighting demons, I ask?

Most of my dreams throughout my years involve just that. Different places, different children, different scenarios, but always the same theme. One of the first dreams that I can remember revolved around where we lived. It was a small townhome community, with a red-brick façade, and one big oval road that you can only enter one way, and leave one way. We lived in an end unit, three bedrooms, one and a half bathrooms, small front yards, and a shared sidewalk with your neighbors. Next to us was a family that I was close with. They had a son and daughter, of which the son was the same age as myself, and we used to hang out, so I was familiar with the layout of their house.

What I remember, of that particular dream, was that I was out front playing, and I just felt this overwhelming dark presence, like something bearing down, yet the sun was still shining, everything appeared normal, and no one else seemed to notice. I just remember feeling panicked and yelling at all of the kids to run, as fast as they could, into my neighbor's house. Why I knew it was a safe haven, I do not know, but as soon as I slammed the front door behind me, there was such a loud bang, like I'd slammed the door on something! God, the feeling, I wish I could put it into words how scared I was, yet angry at the same time. Why would anyone want to hurt those kids? There were about five children, staring wide-eyed at me, so confused, and again, I do not understand WHY I knew that they were in danger, I just did!

Once I gathered the strength to look out the peephole of the front door, nothing was there. All was normal, but I knew if I opened that door, we were all done for. The bang hit the door again, this time, much louder, and at the same time, along the top part of the living room wall, where we all sat, a sign appeared, like the ones you would see at the grocery store or DMV. It was digital, lit up, and did continual scrolling. It went the entire length of the room, around all four corners, and just kept repeating "Give me the children, and you can go free" over and over and over. I just shouted back, "There is no way you are getting these kids, and you will not win!" The screeching that came after my response still gives me chills to this day! I do not know how long we sat there, more threats came, I was now going to die whether I handed the children over or not, but I knew we were safe if we stayed put. Time passed, the heaviness and fear went away, and I just felt that it was over – then I woke up!

Many more dreams would haunt me over the years, but I never thought much of it until I was introduced into the paranormal community, by way of my husband, Chris Allgood. When we started dating in 2011, he would tell me of the ghosts he had been seeing since childhood and asked me if I had ever seen anything or had any experiences. I slowly opened up to him about my dreams, and he talked me through what he believed it may have been, that I possibly could have been astral-planing, or maybe in another lifetime, I was a protector of children. To this day, we have many conversations on what it all could mean.

After some time had passed, and Chris and I had been involved within the paranormal community, there was a deep connection with many of the people I have met along the way and a peace of mind in knowing that I am not alone. I think that is a big relief to many of us, that there is a community of like-minded souls who want to confirm, search, and communicate with others that are not on our same plane.

So whether you are old school and like the recorders, or you have a gift to communicate, or you are advancing forward with technology, like Staticom, we are all of us in this together for the greater good. I, for one, cannot wait to see what the future holds. Happy hunting to all of you, please remember to be courteous, as they are still spirits of one kind or another, be safe, be patient, but remember to "Stay haunted!"

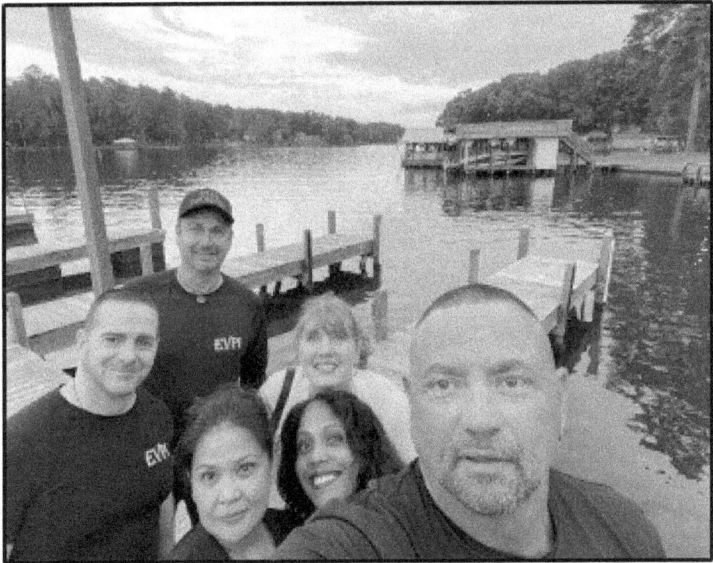

17. Life Is But a Dream?

YES, yes, go ahead and sing it, "Life is but a dream, life is but a dream...doo wop!" I am not old enough to remember when that song came out, but I DID hear it in movies and television shows when I was a kid. I remember a fantastic movie about a boy who became a singer much like his father had been, called *Looking for an Echo*, and it was really good, in my opinion. The original song, performed by The Harptones, was written by songwriters Hy Weiss and Raoul J. Cita. It's a classic and a long-shelf-life tune.

Anyway, this idea put forth by the chapter's title is one rooted in my most recent deep dive into aspects of depth psychology and philosophy with regard to the fantastical works of spirit communication. Whenever I find a new concept, idea or outlook on something, I don't allow it to steamroll my current paradigm and world instantiation, but instead first look for connections to it, conflicts with it, and then look at where I see it going. Support and lack of support for my beliefs and views allow it to organically fit and fail to fit before I begin to jostle pieces around for a fusion that is not forced...

The idea of life actually being a dream state as much as a dream itself is nothing new. Depending on your background and educational experience, you may or may not have heard of it and in varying levels of detail. But if you look at the experiential aspects of life and dreams and the many similarities, some of which can be drawn to states of mind associated with mental disorders, you see that the vividness and feelings drummed up are analogously real to the individual. This blowing off of a materialist-based roof raises many questions with regard to all sorts of things such as astral travel, time slips and more. Perhaps the perceived astral travel does not entail actually traversing any distances as physical sciences would know and measure them. Maybe it is just the quelling of the excitations that usually forge our amplified, self-egoic experience and the accessing or emboldening of the excitations that are integral to the astral experience. Maybe we experience the venturing about, seemingly traversing tremendous distances in a flash, something we would expect in our realm of spirit and its having no space-time to adhere to as well.

Perhaps, as this outlooks suggests, it is true that the dream is NOT in the body (or brain), but the body and all of its neural firings are instead inside the dream. It does make sense that when the excitations of consciousness that bombard us during our waking hours, once quelled by sleep, would give way to the other parts of our psyche that are in fact obfuscated and eclipsed by them. Maybe we don't have the ghost-like soul or essence that vacates the body like a delinquent renter upon the commencement of physical death, but instead, perhaps filters are lifted, and our tuning into the full-blown universal mind or consciousness is now more broadly accessible and experienced, or experienced differently once physical sensory input is not a factor. We do identify with our bodies and physical forms a lot; more than we do our spirit. But, as I've mentioned before and read in many versions, we don't ever say, "I AM a body" – but we do say, "I HAVE a body" – which seems to indicate an innate acceptance or acknowledging of the driver's seat being occupied by mind/consciousness and not its vehicle, being the bodies we have come to know. This is a large part of what I am beginning to see as a viable, truth-based reality.

The more I venture towards an understanding and acceptance of the philosophical view known as "objective idealism," the more I see where some of us actually do hold views that are in fact devoid of bivalence BUT in ways that may conflict in the belief systems they adhere to, like believing in panpsychism and not at the same time. Like being a vegan who eats burgers made of meat once a month. We should all probably continue to delve into what it is we feel and believe and see where the avenues associated with those lead. I am taking things beyond evidence capture in my quest to understand and document paranormality because if there is any factor that may be playing a role, I want to take it into account. I may rule it out brilliantly or foolishly, but unlike the rigid materialist types, I will not simply cast it aside as if it does not exist. So this is why I think knowing the extensions of our beliefs and the continuity is important. Look at it this way, and this likening is odd to me because I am not a very politically minded person at all, but this does remind me of how a politician will attempt to pass a bill, and it will have riders or provisos on it, things that are also enacted if said bill is passed and are often left out of the verbal discussions but, like airbags in cars, went from having to be spoken of if you wanted to include them, to being simply added as a standard feature of the vehicle, be it automotive or political in nature.

I may have written about this before, Lord knows I have said it several times at events and lectures and on podcasts, but it strikes me as odd when we do hold conflicting beliefs but do not seem to know it. One of my prime examples of this, that I have harped on many times, is when we say something about looking for or identifying the frequency spirits are on or using, YET we say the realm of spirit has no space-time as we know it. We completely toss out the fact that frequency is a measurement based on units, or oscillations of time, per second. So how can we determine a frequency in a realm we have no access to, for the most part, and do so trying to pin down a number when the way we usually pin such down involves using a measured unit of time in a realm we believe has NO linear time as we experience it? I feel as if these conflicted situations in the field of paranormal research and investigation are what not only put divides between us but also serve up those divides as vulnerabilities to those who look to show our shortcomings, be it via not following university-level protocols, having a formal enough education, or just applying your garden-variety common sense. We cannot hand the enemy the weapon against us and begrudge them for using it. Our offensive is not against them, it is within us. We fix our issues, we make them reach, dig and stretch to find something to target...and they will. It's their nature to do so, but making it easy is just foolish for us.

I'll give you a strong example of how we uphold a conflict, and so many of us do on this one, yet do not acknowledge both sides that are in opposition at the same time. I've never heard it from anyone. The problem, as you will see in a moment, is that it requires us to resolve it immediately. It mandates reconciliation, OR we are screaming "hypocrisy is my mantra" in realizing and ignoring the need to adjust somewhere between the two sides. Most of us have heard of mobile phone apps being the subject of intense and harsh ridicule. They are not to be trusted; they can record you and repeat words back; they are programmed with loaded words like "demon" or "ghost."

This may be true in many instances. I myself do not think there is a magical app that makes talking to ghosts happen. But if they can work through and with electronics, then to me it seems reasonable that the phone, an electromagnetic device, can also be worked through, and if the app in use is meant to be communicative, then maybe all the more. Radars

153

and such, I am very much unsure of, but leave that to another discussion. So...here's where it gets fun. Ready for the paranormal paradox of the century?

From the same mouths of the masses in the ghost-hunting world, two statements followed by the one conclusion that may uncomfortably tie them together and force that need to reconcile I was talking about before. Ready?

"I do not trust mobile apps. They are not credible."

"I love John Zaffis. He is an icon and authority in the paranormal field."

We all have heard both – but – did you also know...John Zaffis is very fond of using Echovox? For those to whom this is news, it is a mobile phone and tablet app that I myself have seen yield impressive results, especially when Johnny has used it. So how do the masses reconcile having the most respect and trust in a person and not in a method they use? I think this exemplifies what I have always said, that the field and its instances or cases must be ruled upon one at a time and not using any blanket statements. Should one find a universal truth applicable to all instances of a certain means of communication, then so be it. We follow suit with the sufficient amount of evidence of it to make us feel it is such. But beyond that, it is a case-by-case field, I would say. And in accounting for our filter-hypothesis-based mind in consciousness presence and what excitations can pull focus, one not buying into a method may be sufficient to damper or quash its performance. Fascinating how when we see or hear what we "want" to hear, it's our minds at play making the desire so, but when those who oppose anything paranormal existing at all fail to see or experience, it is a copout or mystical woo-woo to suggest that they are closed off or blocking it out. Gotta love those who never see the sharp side of the blade that cuts BOTH ways, they somehow remain impervious, and its impact is dulled on them.

18. Frank-ly Speaking About Spirit

"Beyond Sight" – Written by Frankie Adao, MSW

"A ghost is a human being who has passed out of the physical body, usually in a traumatic state and is usually not aware of his true condition. We are all spirits encased in a physical body. At the time of passing, our spirit body continues into the next dimension. A ghost, on the other hand, due to trauma, is stuck in our physical world and needs to be released to go on." – Hans Holzer

MY JOURNEY (FRANKIE) into the field of paranormal research started at an early age. I am not one of those individuals who come into the field because I have been bestowed a special gift or have communicated with those beyond the living. Having loved the horror genre from a young kid, Hollywood actually gets the credit this time!

Through films like *The Exorcist* and *Poltergeist,* I was open to the belief that some form of existence continued when the physical form expired! The notion that those in my life who have passed on still exist always brought me great comfort. This belief stays with me until the present day!

My belief in the afterlife really went into motion when I entered the field of psychology. My career as a therapist working with individuals who have advanced forms of schizophrenia and schizoaffective disorders planted a seed! I would speak to people about what they would experience having auditory and visual hallucinations, and the accounts were fascinating to me.

Many of the folks I would speak to would tell me that they heard and saw loved ones who have passed on and would speak to them from beyond the grave! This started my desire to know the truth! Is it psychosis or indeed a level of communication with the spirit world that most are unable to tap into or acknowledge?

How do you explain people who do not know each other or are from different cultures and demographics, yet share a common experience? For me, it is not a question of circumstance! I became intrigued by proving the medical model of these disorders wrong! This intrigue led to my fascination with the field of parapsychology!

Going back to being a lover of horror and the thrill of being scared, I would frequent horror attractions and, like many, became obsessed with the feeling of being terrified. I would travel all over to go to the most intense jump-scare attractions! When I had my fill, I started to think about that question of what causes a person to feel like there is something beyond the living?

Through my profession as a therapist working in forensic social work at Rutgers University with individuals with lots of trauma, I started to correlate the living human experience with those who have passed on! This mindset led me to dig into theorists such as J. B. Rhine and Hans Holzer. Great minds that continue to influence my work with spirit.

I wanted to experience hands-on what it felt like to communicate with those who no longer exist on this plane. So I started going on public investigations with ghost tour companies. These tours were important because they started to shape my theory that even in the afterlife, there is a human existence that does not end!

Concepts like highly emotional states like anger and frustration were common with spirit. Trauma was a big commonality as well! This led me to start understanding that the living experience with the afterlife is no different than two living people exchanging an emotional experience! It is a form of communication bridging the living and those who have passed on together.

On Halloween of 2021, I attended an investigation at the infamous White Hill Mansion in Fieldsboro, New Jersey. What better way to celebrate my favorite holiday than an evening with spirit in their element! The story of White Hill Mansion is one rich in history, from the Revolutionary War to the prohibition era and the people who made the mansion their home! Moving through the halls of White Hill, I was immediately connected to the space! It had a pulse! It was almost as if the mansion itself was trying to communicate! To this day White Hill Mansion is one of my favorite places to conduct paranormal research!

On the second floor of the mansion, there is what is called the "creepy bathroom"! The tour guides who work at White Hill and keep up the restoration of the sprawling home recommend we sit and do some observations in the white cast-iron, clawfoot tub in the bathroom. Naturally I did.

In the beginning stages of my paranormal research endeavors, I had no equipment or tools! No fancy gizmos or gadgets! Just my own thoughts, feelings and experiences. While sitting in this tub, I heard yelling and commotion coming from the first floor! I jumped out of the tub, headed downstairs, when halfway down the stairs, I stopped to observe what was a gentleman claiming he was being pinned down physically by a spirit entity! I was fully intrigued with the situation! It was just what I was waiting for! Spirit interacting with the living! Good for me! Bad for that poor gentleman!

While sitting on the stairs, I had a perfect view of the man claiming he was being held hostage by an unknown entity. I quickly became fascinated not just by what I was witnessing, but how everyone in the room was responding and reacting to what was happening! It was a perfect storm of psychological impacts on those in the main foyer of the house.

I just so happened to be behind a gentleman standing on the staircase. He was holding an SLS camera (which I only saw on ghost-hunting shows) and picking up what appeared to be an entity standing on the man lying on the floor! It was super tall! There was no way possible that the man being pinned down could see what was being picked up by the SLS, yet he described where this entity was applying pressure to specific parts of his body. It matched up to what we were seeing on the SLS camera! The night and investigation ended, and I headed home INSPIRED!

At that time, I was doing a podcast called *The UnNormalized Podcast*, where I spoke to people about their experiences and journeys in life. I started to do episodes where I covered dark history. Naturally, I wanted to do an episode on my White Hill Mansion experience. I was determined to get that gentleman's SLS footage I had been watching on the stairs at the mansion on Halloween!

I scoured the socials and came across the Friends of White Hill Mansion Facebook page. Lo and behold, there it was... THE SLS FOOTAGE!

I immediately reached out to the gentleman, whose name was Anthony Manatrizio, and explained to him how I had been standing behind him that evening, watching him capture this extraordinary phenomenon! I asked if I could use the footage in my podcast episode, and he generously said yes! To this day, that episode still gets high views, as it is compelling footage! The days that followed the Halloween investigation at White Hill Mansion stayed with me and fueled my desire to truly connect this physical world with the realm beyond the veil!

There was an overwhelming pull to again reach out to Anthony, the gentleman whose SLS footage I borrowed, and ask him if he would be interested in doing some research together and starting a paranormal team. He said YES. That was the start of what we now call...THE PARASIGHT EXPERIENCE. Anthony is my partner and co-founder. My brother in paranormal research! He, a seasoned law enforcement officer, and I, a therapist in the field of forensic psychology for Rutgers University, were the perfect partnership! That partnership led to a lasting brotherhood beyond the paranormal!

Our mission at ParaSight is simple: taking the field of paranormal research and using our skills to conduct our own credible paranormal research! We use a combination of scientific methods and parapsychology to do the work with spirit! I have done many things in my life that have been amazing experiences, but creating ParaSight, working with Anthony and our team, is one of my proudest achievements!

We have investigated some of the tristate area's most notorious locations! Our team works closely with some of the paranormal field's finest names! The ParaSight team is dynamic in the way that we tap into the skill sets of each member! Anthony has developed a research method called the Manatrizio experience grading system (MEGS). In simple terms, MEGS is an experiential observation grading system where we take our captures and categorize them by anecdotal and empirical evidence. This helps us collect data and aids in our research validity. We marry that with concepts from my experience in therapy working from a trauma-based modality. In addition, Anthony is the team's tech guru! Building ITC devices and equipment such as his EMPT box, which uses electromagnetic proximity sensors to detect activity! He even has me build some tech, most of which never works, so I understand principles of how technology and devices work in the field.

Understanding trauma with spirit is a very important aspect of why I do the work! When we get reports of experiences of physical or intense interaction from spirit, we look at that outreach from beyond the veil as secondary responses to primary emotions. Responses such as rage, aggression, irritation, withdrawing, anxiety, and fear stem from primary emotions such as sadness, anger, guilt, shame and trauma attachment.

My approach to working with spirit is to understand what their experiences are like both from their physical time in this dimension and their time that exists beyond the veil. I started using a technique I call parapsychological desensitization reprocessing (PDR). It is a derivative of Dr. Francine Shapiro's eye movement desensitization reprocessing (EMDR) form of therapy.

In the EMDR modality of evidence-based treatment, you are using bilateral stimulation and eye movement to mimic the neurobiological state of the REM stage of sleep. It is during the REM sleep-like state that we can slow down the overstimulated amygdala part of the brain and sync brain waves with repro-processing traumatic memories or events. EMDR has been highly effective in treating trauma and PTSD.

My version of this evidence-based therapeutic modality, PDR, comes from a perspective that there is consciousness after physical death! If spirits are communicating using either primary or secondary emotions (that normally derive in the living and are processed in the limbic system of the brain), consciousness and brain activity in the afterlife in theory has to exist! How else would spirit be able to intelligently respond with primary and secondary emotional responses to their situations?

PDR uses Shapiro's principles of EMDR to help spirit repro-process trauma. Through an eight-phase process, PDR allows me to communicate with spirit from a therapeutic lens. It is my hope that using the PDR modality will help spirits heal their trauma using bilateral stimulation and aid in their "crossing over."

Team ParaSight also is joined by a valued team member, Jennie Collucci, who is also a Rutgers University alumni in the field of science and chemistry. Jennie's approach to working with spirit comes from her principles of marrying "science and sensitivity"! Looking at the work with spirit from a scientific method but with a sensitive approach to spirit's experiences with tremendous respect. It is a guiding principle we use to do our work!

Our team is composed of scientists, law enforcement, therapists, mediumship and genuine care for spirit. Team ParaSight conducts parapsychological research in locational environments, conducting scientific studies in the most notorious paranormal locations such as Pennhurst Asylum, the historical Betsy Ross House in Philadelphia, Cresson Sanitarium, Hinsdale House, Burlington County Jail, White Hill Mansion, the Shanley Hotel, the Old 76 House Tavern, the 1890s House, and more! We also work with private clients to bridge communications between families and spirit. Team ParaSight has a residency location where we host public and private investigations at the haunted Ritz Theatre in Haddon Township, New Jersey. A theater whose history dates back to the vaudeville era and even has ties to being an adult movie house in the '70s. It is a fascinating and special place! Our connection to the spirits at the Ritz is a bond that comes from their trust in our team! The proceeds from our work at the Ritz go right back to the theater to keep performing arts programming alive in our community!

We continue to do the work with spirit while developing our approaches to understand and communicate from that "science and sensitivity" perspective! It is our goal and continued commitment to spirit!

– Author's Note: Frankie and his team made an undeniably awesome impression on many of us when we first worked with them as special guests for their Ritz Theater debut event. Truly the finest of people. We love them all...Frankie, Jennie, Anthony, Paul, etc.

19. If It's All in My Head, Why Am I Not Making It Easy?!

THERE ARE so many things that we take at face value. We just accept them. They are in a way, if not entirely, axioms. But sometimes, my semi-pro philosopher and pro-level satirist looks at phrases, sayings, words, metaphors, etc. and wonders why the thinking of analytical interpretation of them is incomplete or, at times, nonexistent.

Think about this concept for a moment...

Oftentimes we're told that seeing and hearing paranormal phenomena is "all in our heads." We're the unwitting victims of trickery and charades that originate in our own heads and brains. The things that our cynics apply this to are productive intentioned acts such as our positive interpreting of audio or video data as evidence of the unknown. So let's start here... intent tied to an act or decision, to my knowledge, has not yet been proven to flip-flop mid-act. Given that reasonable assumption, if we begin interpreting data for the positive intent purpose we do, we will be sticking with that same intention, seeing it through to completion or whenever we wrap it up.

With me so far? Ok – good. Moving on...

In our assessment of data, figuring out if and what words we hear (with class A being not much to figure out as much as make note of), it struck me as odd that we often have to spend more time, analysis, peer input, etc. on determining what we've got as would-be evidence. So if it is our brains (mind=consciousness in my view, so it's not the same as one's brain), why would we not make what we "believe" we hear clear-cut and final in an instant? Why interpret at all? Why try to figure out anything? Yes, our language, for us English, is ambiguous in its nature with things such as "no" and "know" spelled differently, with different meanings and use yet audibly identical. So context would come into play when assessing evidence capture, which for me was always the case and akin to timing and relevance in deciding its final outcome to be logged. So why not assign context and what the words are without any problem-solving or need to deliberate at all if this is all the creation of neural firings and thought formations?

If there is a biochemical, biological or purely physical flaw in hearing that leads to so many miscues and misinterpretations of what we perceive to be voices of spirit – if they are perhaps no more than warbles and artifacts of sound – why don't our minds streamline, simplify and make it all understandable, and at speeds and cadences familiar to us all? When someone sees the Virgin Mary's face in a cloud formation or grilled cheese sandwich, it's pareidolia – making sense out of chaos where no sense actually exists – so why, if what I hear is also ALL in my head, do I leave a modicum of challenge in puzzle-solving in the equation? – if we're going to create a narrative and cohesive sentences within our mind, why not do so with supreme certainty as to what is being said? People often think what we hear or annotate hearing was noted after one listen and a diluted state of comprehension failure. We often decide via context when a word or more is close between more than one syllabic possibility. SO...Why speculative or oftentimes divided between two or three words? Why quicker than humans can talk? Why off speed/cadence? Why poetic shorthand and not full sentences all of the time? How does the process used for ITC affect the interpretation or result if the result is birthed from neural synapses and not consciousness and our self-reflective egoic experience? That is continuity of thought!

Any other instance(s), studies that show any other sensory-processing situation within which our cognitive functionality involved complicated things, or made them more muddy? Not sure I know of any, so please tell me if such exists. I understand the probability of needing to solve something, figure it out, but if the illusion is self-generated and not being played ON us, but rather, BY us, why would we make it hard? Would we not just leap-frog to a conclusion of absolute certainty quickly and waste no time on solving it? Again, this is not meant to be a clinical chapter but a thought-provoking one, because it seems counterintuitive and bizarre to me that we would work against ourselves if we're tricking ourselves. And if we are and do, HOW can we know and tell when it is ok to trust our senses? Are there limits, boundaries or necessary aspects to when it can happen? Can our brains trick us into showing up for work on time at our spouse's or girlfriend's job instead of our own? At a job we were fired from, the next day we leave the house for work in the morning? Why not? We are already, according to team cynic, making ourselves see and hear ghosts and spirits? A little navigational trickery seems modest enough in comparison?

Doesn't this whole idea seem to be in direct conflict with the weapon of choice for most all cynics and snooty academics alike?...Pareidolia!

With their plague-level, rampant pareidolia dismissal of audio "would-be" evidence, it is our mind trying to make sense out of nonsense, identifying patterns or trying to finish what appears to be a pattern. So this to me shows a trend toward completing and simplification. Making something that we can digest and know with comfortable familiarity versus staying stuck in a mystery. So...if we look to make things best for our understanding, and that is why we think we're getting intelligent communication, then why doesn't our brain and/or mind (no, they're not the same thing) just jump to the most logical and close to how it sounds explanation and be done with it? Why leave it in many if not MOST instances something to decipher and figure out? If that is actually what can be clinically proven, what data supports that, and what is suggested as to why we fabricate so inefficiently if we're looking to just solve something? Don't get me wrong, I am not saying there isn't any level of this happening. But what I am saying is one cannot blanket statement it out and not know why other than that it supports their paradigm of doubt and has no truth-value in it, thus, must be bull-caca.

This to me suggests we're doing two things that our mind and brains do daily and quite well...identifying speech to pay attention to and trying to understand what is being said...but words being said, not the question. THAT we know is the case. Think about this for a moment. Do we ever truly try to interpret a dog bark or cat meow? We do not. But we do try to interpret and understand their behaviors because those, we have come to realize, are viable means of communicating with us for them. See my point? Just trying to provoke thought here...

We process and attempt to understand, in the language that we know...language...words...speech...talking. Can sounds, which build our words bit by bit, be misinterpreted as words? YES. Does it happen? YES! But if someone is trying to state that at the rate of recorded anomalous data thought to be intelligent speech, meaning how much of it is captured as often as it is, these proponents of pareidolia are suggesting explain one hundred percent of it (or close to that amount), then they NEED (in my humble opinion)...NEED to show data that suggests this hearing and interpreting deficiency is not limited to purely paranormal instances...OR...they are baseless and unfounded as extreme as those who tried to claim covid variants were targeting people in red or blue states as if a calculated plan being carried out by a partisan virus. See how bizarre that sounds? Know why? IT IS.

20. Artificial Intelligence and the Chinese Room

What We Need to Understand as AI Enters Paranormal Research

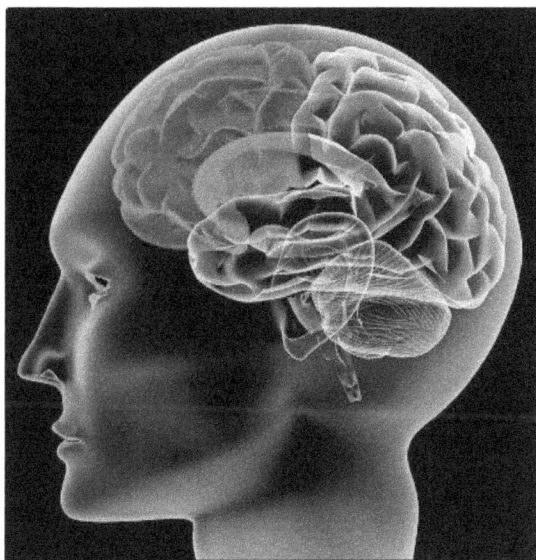

WE ALL HEAR IT NOWADAYS...ARTIFICIAL intelligence is going to take jobs, lives, resources and ultimately control of this world. Perhaps. I do not pretend to be educated or experienced enough to determine a probable outcome in such extreme pathways, but I do think that we can all posit more educated guesses if we understand some of what not just technology, but philosophy (there is that word again) tell us.

First off, what in the world is a Chinese room? Like in a Chinese restaurant? "Are you writing this while you are hungry?" you may be asking me here. No, well, yes, but no... that is not why I wrote those words in the title. I'll explain... after I order dinner. Damn that power of suggestion; got me again (this jest gets clearer in the next chapter).

The Chinese room was actually a thought experiment done in order to determine if a machine or mechanism actually understands things or just simulates what appears to be an understanding. This thought experiment was the main focus of philosopher John Searle in his paper "Minds, Brains, and Programs," published in *Behavioral and Brain Sciences* in 1980.

Searle's thought experiment began with a hypothetical premise that asked the question, does a machine, any machine with the ability to learn, literally comprehend Chinese? Or is it merely simulating an ability to understand it?

In our era of AI and its emergence into games, writing, music production and more, this is an ever-present concern for many. Rumors and fearmongering ideas about artificial intelligence taking everything over are already creeping across the globe. Movies and television are, no question, catalysts for this movement. It's what they do when they entertain. Keeping that in mind, if you can't already tell, I am not worried about this so much, because this research teaches us a valuable lesson. Hear me out...

Let us say, in a not-difficult-to-imagine scenario, that artificial intelligence research succeeds in producing a computer, or even more extreme, mass produces them, and it behaves as if it is fluent in and totally understands Chinese. It runs with Chinese characters via input, carries out instructions and protocols of a computer program, and produces other Chinese characters, which it advances this process to then present as its yielded work. Mr. Searle then asks, "What IF this computer performs its tasks so convincingly that it seems to prove out that it also passes the Turing test?" This test, by the way, is one that basically determines if a machine's displayed intellect is equal to and indistinguishable from human intellect. Can and does it convince a person who is of Chinese descent that the program is itself an actual live Chinese speaker?

In short form, the Chinese room argument says that it is possible for a system to simulate intelligence without actually being intelligent. Whereas the Turing test says that if a system can simulate intelligence, then it actually is intelligent. Does this feel like it has the same appeal as the bivalence discussed in this book as well? Perhaps. Could it be both? Who can say for sure? Back on task...

For every question put forth, it yields an appropriate response. It is reasonable to assume that any human being who is genuinely fluent in Chinese would be convinced that they are interacting with another Chinese-speaking human being.

The takeaway, according to Mr. Searle, is that there is no necessary difference between the roles of the computer and the person who executes the tasks in the Chinese room, in the experiment. Each simply follows a program, step-by-step, producing behavior that is then interpreted by the user as evidence of intelligent conversation. The fascinating and beyond noteworthy distinction is that the individual inside the Chinese room, which was Searle himself, would not be able to understand an actual conversation...as he pointed out, saying, "I don't speak a word of Chinese."

Therefore, Searle then proclaims, it makes sense and seems in concert that the computer would not be able to understand a conversation in Chinese, either.

Searle suggests, and to me this is quite convincing, that without an actual understanding or intentionality, we cannot depict what the instrument is doing as taking part in cognitive thought or, in a word, thinking, and since it does not actually think, it does not have a mind as we identify the term. Consequently, he concludes, basically saying, the AI is not mirroring every facet of human mind and sentience.

Additionally, Gottfried Leibniz, a German philosopher, mathematician, scientist and diplomat, made a similar argument as far back as the year 1714! This is nothing new conceptually, as we begin to realize. His position of opposition, by the way, was against this humanity-based idea of mechanism (the idea that everything that makes up a human being could, in principle, be explained in mechanical terms. In other words, a person, including their mind, is merely a very complex machine.

There is an increasingly larger need to have a viable philosophy as much or more so than just a technical understanding of ITC and spirit communication, the more I understand how it dresses, frames and sets the stage for all else we proclaim to believe and execute in experimental instances. We have to understand the ontological platform upon which our beliefs, logic and even basis for our evidence actually rest.

A fair brushing up on terms would lead me back to a place I find digestible and accessible definitions that are not overexplained. So Wikipedia it is...

According to Wikipedia.com...in metaphysics, ontology is the philosophical study of being, as well as related concepts such as existence, becoming, and reality. Think of how impactful this is to not only convey to others but to yourself, your positions behind your assessments and evidence that go beyond the worldview science and the laws of sound that cynics who have no actual philosophy use against you. You are in a veritable Roman coliseum, and the double-edged axe is a weapon that you or your opponent may use...this is analogous to the use of language, laws and theory when the arena remains the same, the one the cynics are able to grab the same weapons within and turn them on you. And even then, if you do not know your stuff, you go down for the count.

21. Annotations, Assumptions and A-holes

Abuse in the Use of the Idiom "Power of Suggestion"

I HATE SPEAKING TO HIM

ANY OF US who have spent any time in the field of paranormal research or ghost hunting oftentimes also find themselves looking to share and post evidence clips we've captured and deemed worthy of consumption by others. Nothing wrong with that, to me. We even showcase such when we guest on podcasts that broadcast in video. When we do this with audio evidence, aka spirit vocal captures, we (most of us) caption or annotate the words on the screen as part of the presentation making of it. Again, to me, nothing wrong with that. Some do not like to view the words on screen when first hearing audio evidence; some do not care; to me that is a choice, as some mediums do not like to know any history prior to entering a location, while some do not mind. Same deal for me on this...not seeing anything wrong with it. But...is it creating a subjective experience? Is it influential or a confirmation of auditory sense input or both?

What is the power of annotation?

A proper and concise online definition says..."Annotations are a critical strategy teachers can use to encourage students to interact with a text. They promote a deeper understanding of passages and encourage students to read with a purpose."

In psychology, what are the core elements of suggestion?

Much of my research into this online provided three consistent components for suggestion and its power:

1. the introduction of an idea into the brain
2. the acceptance of the idea, and...
3. the realization of the idea.

It seems what the annotating types are on trial for is fudging the authenticity of the outcome of line 2 above. Acceptance of the idea. Introduction and realization seem unaffected by our putting words on a screen, but that acceptance part...ah, there's the rub!

If the societal worldviews such as the most recent "Me too" movement are the mass implementation of the power of suggestion, is not a keen awareness of such and skepticism towards content that may be averse to one's core beliefs – such as paranormality – be as persuasive and influential as the allegedly leading annotated words on the screen, showing the spoken words within the evidence clip? Would this not offset and balance out the cynic-minded folks who see words on paranormal audio file videos and already say, "I don't hear any of that"? And at what point does this power of sugges- tion, one that is not fueled by something akin to solar panels, run out of steam, momentum and no longer push us far afield, off base in our accurately assessing ANYTHING? Yet we often hear, especially when showing evidence video clips to those NOT in the field, that we're trying to make them hear what we hear.

Captioning or annotating is "leading" people to hear what you hear, and thus, once they arrive at this judgment, they find such to be discrediting?! You know what it seems no one factors in at that time? How about my credibility and experi- ence, and when I heard it and I annotated it? I DID NOT have words on the screen. I heard that caca by myself and without a second thought. Clear as day!

Believe it or not, directed especially towards team cynic, the main reason any of us have and do annotate the evidence file videos we make is because we are disclosing what WE HAVE heard. People still say they hear it, full, partly or not at all.

If we harken back to chapter one and the battle of personal sensory systems, we can look at this even deeper. It is my academic layperson opinion, with the application of what I find to be common sense and continuity of thought, that this concept is overly leaned on with the words and their perceived power of suggestion, because if the probability was not there, that "power" wouldn't be either. We cannot audio describe a helicopter and convince someone what we saw and just described is a tricycle. If it busts out beyond what our reasoning knows to be viable and with little to no truth-based value, we cannot expect it to carry the sway it so loosely gets assigned capable of, at all.

Then secondly, the wording cadence, tone and phonetic quality have to be related to like-sounding words or that "power" is not going to override its suggestive properties either. It can't make the word tree sound like asphyxiation.

And lastly, purely from an ITC and pure white-noise application standpoint, devoid of any data, the fact that words are present to be agreed upon, argued over or misconstrued is itself fantastical because in these settings, no words or speech should be present at all. So if you hear no OR know – hair OR hare, etc. – that is already anomalous and amazing.

And how limited or not IS this suggestive power we have over ourselves or that others can have over us in any aspect of reality interpretation and assessment? What if senses are impaired or others heightened or both? Can we use closed captions with the deaf and make them think they're watching *The Waltons* when it is actually *The Jeffersons*? Yes, they can see the differences, but if the words being present on screen are capable of overriding the auditory properties of hearing the sounds, phonetics and assembly of speech-building blocks, making people hear what is not there, or heck...not even speech...just good ole artifacts and warbles of sound, then why not make them see *The Waltons* as *The Jeffersons*... unless what you're thinking is that it could not happen because their perceived truth-value in SEEING the people is a value greater than their perceptibility to read these jargon, slang and cultural speech differences. What if the language was indicative of country folk, city folk or somewhere else with no visual element at all? Would we then be able to lead people to build a visual picture as to who and where the scene is taking place?

Are we arriving at the determination that sight trumps sound but reading trumps sound too but not in the presence of conflicting information via sight? See how continuity is the easiest way to stay consistent in beliefs and theory?

Interestingly, as I am wrapping up the writing of this fourth book, Lourdes pushed to see an experiment done with regard to this whole superpower of suggestion. It panned out as expected, so I felt it pertinent to include it here before this book goes to print. What did she have in mind? It was a basic but sound experiment that removes any potential for one to say it was leading or suggestive but rather, authentic in what people report.

In a nutshell, we recorded a few Staticom-based vocals that, to us, were so freaking clear that she wanted us to send the video with audio out to a dozen trusted paranormal investigators and researchers and see if they hear what we heard or not and WITHOUT any annotated words included in the video. So we did just that...

Other than the opening word, which itself may have been determined or led by context, the responses from all of those who heard it were the same. This speaks to the possibilities suggestion CAN have, as the one thing that may have (not certain) been influential was including the question asked during that Staticom sitting at the Red Mill Museum in Clinton New Jersey. This we do because without context, you may have an anomalous voice, but a response, an intelligent response, now THAT is made clear when you hear the question. In this case, it may have influenced what people heard from "I'm standing in the light" to "They're standing in the light" – with that question from a guest of the event having been, "Are your children there with you?" This can easily be speaking to the "with you" part of it, suggesting a response of where the "standing with you" would even be...in the light. Or it can be saying where the children inquired about are at this point in our time.

Suggestion is the psychological process by which a person guides their own or another person's desired thoughts, feelings, and behaviors by presenting stimuli that may elicit them as reflexes instead of relying on conscious effort. So go on right now, buy all of my books, my friend's books and then forget what you did and buy them all again. No? Not working? Ok, so I'll have to practice and add more visuals...

About the Author

Co-host of Entity Voices Paranormal Evidence Podcast (UN-X Network

Author of "*Paranormally Speaking: Knowingly Talking to the Unknown*", "*ITC Techno-mancy: The Magical World of Electronic Spirit Communication*" and "TDSi: The Digital Seance initiative"

Member of the SPR: Society of Psychical Research, Cambridge, UK 2022

Member of Academia.edu / Philosopher / Satirist

Four-time author Ron Yacovetti is living in his home state of New Jersey. However, he began investigating the paranormal during his 14 years as a resident of Los Angeles, California. This geographic diversity gave him the opportunity to investigate some of the most notable haunts on both coasts.

He has a unique background as a stand-up comedian, a writer, and Paranormal Investigator. Ron's background with satire, along with this empirical experience, has shaped his philosophical view of the absurd and paranormal. He applies a keen sense of awareness when hypocrisy and a lack of continuity of thought pervade the paranormal landscape. He is truly the cynic's, cynic.

Over years of research into audio phenomena, Ron believes we need to not only focus more on the study of consciousness, but also Philosophy, if we are to ever influence the reductionist science world instantiation and open up genuine acceptance to the reality of these inexplicable events the world over.

And while Ron enjoys all aspects of investigating, his affinity and area of specificity in the afterlife research was almost instantly discovered in the area known as ITC: Instrumental Trans-Communication. Most know ITC from a variety of devices seen on TV such as the Spirit Box or Ghost Boxes.

Ron continues doing innovative afterlife research and experimentation rooted in the European methodology of ITC known as DRV: DIRECT RADIO VOICE which through the removal of any radio has evolved into what he, Lourdes Gonzalez, Tony and Cherie Rathman now call "The Staticom Project" - producing anomalous vocals out of pure white noise.

facebook.com/ron.yacovetti
x.com/Yacman1
instagram.com/Yacman1

Also by Ron Yacovetti

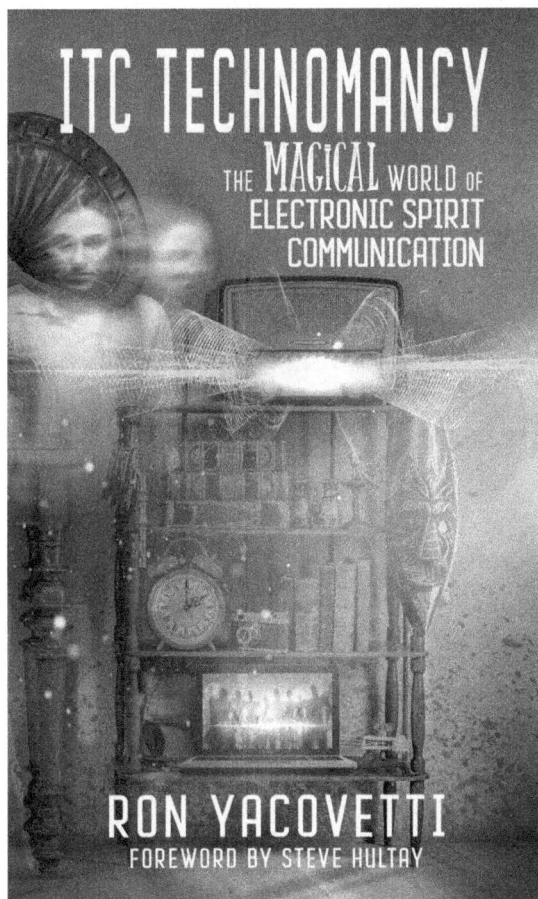

ITC Technomancy: The Magical World of
Electronic Spirit Communication

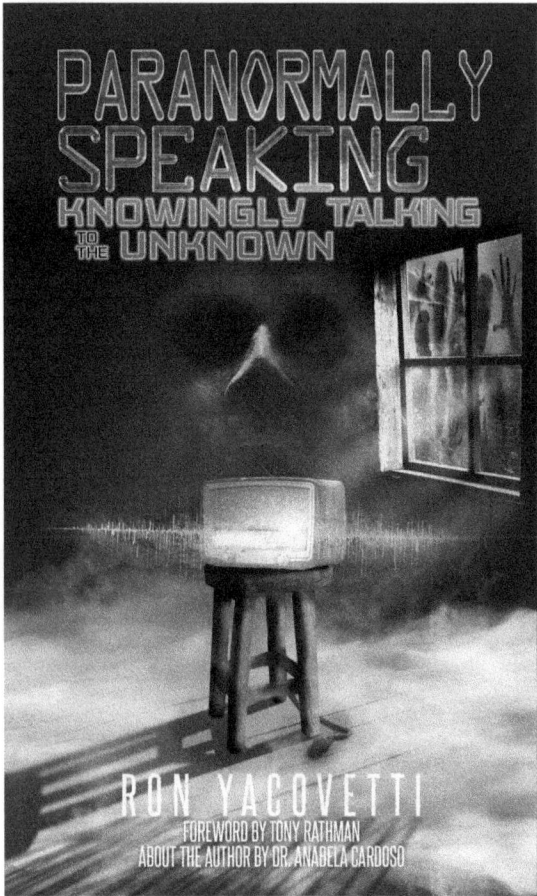

Paranormally Speaking: Knowingly Talking to the Unknown

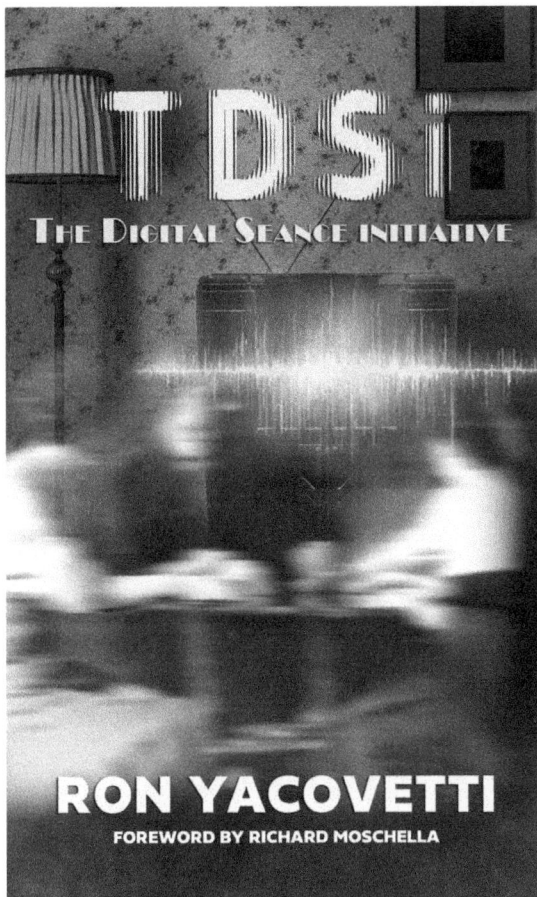

TDSI: The Digital Seance Initiative

www.ingramcontent.com/pod-product-compliance
Lightning Source LLC
Chambersburg PA
CBHW032350280326
41935CB00008B/520